D1525379

JUSTICE BETWEEN THE YOUNG AND THE OLD

OXFORD ETHICS SERIES

Series Editor: Derek Parfit, All Souls College, Oxford

The Limits of Morality
Shelly Kagan

Perfectionism
Thomas Hurka

Inequality
Larry S. Temkin

Morality, Mortality, Volume I
Death and Whom to Save from It
F. M. Kamm

Morality, Mortality, Volume II
Rights, Duties, and Status
F. M. Kamm

Suffering and Moral Responsibility
Jamie Mayerfeld

Moral Demands in Nonideal Theory
Liam B. Murphy

The Ethics of Killing: Problems at the Margins of Life
Jeff McMahan

Intricate Ethics: Rights, Responsibilities, and Permissible Harm
F.M. Kamm

Rethinking the Good: Moral Ideals and the Nature of Practical Reasoning
Larry S. Temkin

The Moral Target: Aiming at Right Conduct in War and Other Conflicts
F.M. Kamm

Justice Between the Young and the Old
Dennis McKerlie

JUSTICE BETWEEN THE
YOUNG AND THE OLD

Dennis McKerlie

OXFORD
UNIVERSITY PRESS

OXFORD

UNIVERSITY PRESS

Oxford University Press is a department of the University of Oxford.
It furthers the University's objective of excellence in research, scholarship,
and education by publishing worldwide.

Oxford   New York
Auckland   Cape Town   Dar es Salaam   Hong Kong   Karachi
Kuala Lumpur   Madrid   Melbourne   Mexico City   Nairobi
New Delhi   Shanghai   Taipei   Toronto

With offices in
Argentina   Austria   Brazil   Chile   Czech Republic   France   Greece
Guatemala   Hungary   Italy   Japan   Poland   Portugal   Singapore
South Korea   Switzerland   Thailand   Turkey   Ukraine   Vietnam

Oxford is a registered trademark of Oxford University Press
in the UK and certain other countries.

Published in the United States of America by
Oxford University Press
198 Madison Avenue, New York, NY 10016

© Oxford University Press 2013

All rights reserved. No part of this publication may be reproduced, stored in a
retrieval system, or transmitted, in any form or by any means, without the prior
permission in writing of Oxford University Press, or as expressly permitted by law,
by license, or under terms agreed with the appropriate reproduction rights organization.
Inquiries concerning reproduction outside the scope of the above should be sent to the
Rights Department, Oxford University Press, at the address above.

You must not circulate this work in any other form
and you must impose this same condition on any acquirer.

Library of Congress Cataloging-in-Publication Data
McKerlie, Dennis.
Justice between the young and the old / Dennis McKerlie.
p. cm.
ISBN 978–0–19–976913–1 (alk. paper)
1. Intergenerational relations.   2. Social justice.   I. Title.
HM726.M397 2012
303.3'72—dc23
2012000400

ISBN 978–0–19–976913–1

3 5 7 9 8 6 4 2
Printed in the United States of America
on acid-free paper

303.372
M157j

To my mother and father

CONTENTS

Acknowledgments   ix

1. Introduction   1
2. Complete Lives Egalitarianism   21
3. The Prudential Lifespan Account   33
4. Equality   52
5. Priority   88
6. Personal Identity and Prudence   118
7. Changes in Values over Time   146
8. Alzheimer's Disease   173
9. Conclusion   197

Index   217

ACKNOWLEDGMENTS

I would like to acknowledge numerous people for their intellectual influence and personal helpfulness. Even though present circumstances make it impossible for me to recall them all, there are many who deserve special notice. Richard Arneson, Norman Daniels, Tom Hurka, Agnieszka Jaworska, Jeff McMahan, Derek Parfit, Seana Shiffrin, and Larry Temkin have, through their work provided me with continual insight and inspiration. Conversations with Risa Kawchuk and Alex Sager helped me to clarify my ideas. Ann Levey, Ruth Michaels, Denise Retzlaf, and Merlette Schnell have given me invaluable assistance and encouragement. Finally, John Baker, who has been a warm and welcome philosophical presence throughout my intellectual life, merits special mention. I thank them all.

JUSTICE BETWEEN THE YOUNG AND THE OLD

Chapter 1

Introduction

1.1 SUPPORT FOR THE ELDERLY

This book is about justice between the young and the old. To focus the discussion it will consider some important social institutions that distribute resources, and, consequently, benefits and harms, among people of different ages.

I hope that it will offer a persuasive general theory of justice between the young and the old. The theory will remain true to the moral complexity of the subject. Any acceptable theory should acknowledge that there are different reasons, and fundamentally different kinds of reasons, relevant to this type of justice. The tendency to suppose that, ultimately, there is only one kind of relevant reason is a problem in the public and political debate about the institutions that I discuss, one that undermines more theoretical attempts to develop principles of justice specifically for age groups and generations.

The facts that generate the issues are fundamental ones, and they have been the subject of much philosophical thought outside moral philosophy. It does not require a reading of Marcel Proust to convince us that our lives are lived in time. We are born at one moment and die at another, and in between we grow older. When we think reflectively about our own lives, we recognize ourselves at different ages, passing through the characteristic temporal stages of a human life. We think of ourselves as living at different times when we think prospectively about what the rest of our lives will be like, and we acknowledge the same facts in a different way when we are old and reflect with satisfaction or regret on the past.

We face these facts in perhaps an even more emotionally powerful form in the lives of the people we care most about. We see our children mature, and we witness the old age and death of our parents. Outside the context of the family, we see the members of different generations and age groups living under common institutions and laws, and faring well or badly.

The nature of time, the nature of personal identity, and the significance of the passage of time for rationality and morality are all potentially relevant to the ethical questions that I discuss. I will consider these broader issues when they seem to me to bear directly on the question I am discussing. However, I do not believe that we need to give a philosophical account of time and of personal identity before we speak to the issue of justice between the young and the old. The success or failure of this book will be a test of the merits of a more direct approach.

It is prosaic but useful to begin by clarifying terms. The word *generation* is ambiguous. I will use it in its most common sense, to refer to a group of people born at roughly the same time. In that sense, Baby Boomers are an example of a particular generation. The important fact about a generation understood in this way is that people remain members of the same generation throughout their lives. Boomers grow old, but they can never outgrow being Baby Boomers. Some writers refer to this sense of generation by the more technical term *birth cohort*. Much later in this book I will take up the problem, which some people think is crucial, of distinguishing between, or individuating, different generations.

By contrast, the term *age group* refers to people who are in the same temporal stage of life. The elderly are an example of an age group. On an individual basis, a person remains a member of the same generation from birth to death but becomes, in turn, a member of each of the different age groups as he passes through the stages of youth, maturity, and old age. Considered collectively, a particular generation first constitutes the age group of the young, then that of the mature, and finally that of the elderly.

For the sake of later discussion I will briefly describe two issues that involve serious public concern about this kind of justice.

The first is about the operation of public pension systems for retirees such as the Canada Pension Plan and American Social Security (for convenience, I will refer to such programs as *social security*, although that term is often given a broader sense). These programs are characteristic of the twentieth-century welfare state. They collect and distribute much more money than programs that are typically considered as welfare programs in the narrow sense: programs intended to redistribute resources from the well-off to the badly-off or to those unable to support themselves. Also, the way in which the social security system is managed has a significant effect on the overall economy. It impacts our lives in ways that go beyond its explicit system of contributions and benefits.

Participation in these programs is usually compulsory. To oversimplify, the programs are financed in a "pay as you go" manner. Revenue is collected from workers and employers by a payroll deduction (or tax), and then distributed to retirees in the form of a pension. This—of course intentionally—has the effect of transferring resources from a later generation to an earlier generation, and from a younger age group to an older age group.[1]

Historically, almost all generations have benefited from their participation in these institutions, in that the economic value of what they received from the institution exceeded, sometimes greatly so, what they contributed to it, taking into account both contributions and benefits over their lives as temporal wholes. It is well known that this state of affairs is unlikely to continue in the future, unless the terms of the institutions are restructured. Because of economic and demographic change, many members of the current generation of young adults seem likely to be net losers through their participation in the institution.

This raises a question of justice. Is it fair that those other generations should benefit when a particular generation is obligated to bear part of the burden of providing their benefits and is also required to accept a loss itself? This concern is not just a matter of worrying about the legitimacy of an inequality. In this case, the inequality between generations is directly caused by the operation of a public institution, one that individuals are required to participate in.

The second and more complicated issue is health care. In Canada, medical care, in general, is publicly funded. In the United States that is not the case, though the medical expenses of retirees are publicly funded under the Medicare program. Revenue is

---

1. This is only one way of managing the system of transfers. I will not discuss which would be best. I will be writing about general moral values that are relevant to social security. Readers who wish to understand the details of the transfers should see *Intergenerational Justice*, Axel Gosseries and Lukas H. Meyer, eds. (Oxford, UK: Oxford University Press, 2009).

collected through a combination of targeted payroll deductions and general taxation, so the bulk of the revenue comes from workers. Medical care is disproportionately consumed by the elderly, especially when we consider acute care (protection against life-threatening disease) and institutional care (long stays in hospitals and nursing homes). Although we do not typically think of the health care system in these terms, in practice it involves a significant transfer of resources from the young to the old and from a later generation to an earlier one.

This transfer raises its own issues of justice. As the elderly come to constitute a larger proportion of the total population or at least of the adult population, the cost of providing them with high-quality acute care and long-term institutional care will become more onerous. The achievements of modern medicine make the problem worse. They enable more people to live to reach old age, and those who are elderly to live to even greater ages, while providing powerful but sometimes extremely costly ways of fighting life-threatening diseases.

Faced with this escalating burden, the members of younger age groups might decide to strictly ration acute care for the elderly and to switch the burden of supporting the elderly in nursing homes from the public to individual families. Would it be fair for the other age groups to refuse to meet the basic health needs of the elderly?

The problem about health care will be more difficult to solve than the problem about social security. In this context, by "solving" I simply mean finding a solution that at least seems reasonable and is one that people can politically agree to and implement; but social security is a purer case of transfers between generations and age groups, so it is the example I will return to most frequently.

1.2 A PUZZLE AND RESPONSES TO THE PUZZLE

However, we cannot move immediately to proposing answers to these two issues of justice. There is a general problem to be considered first: It is not clear how we should think when we raise questions about justice between generations and between age groups.

An example is the best way of illustrating the problem. Suppose that we compare the current circumstances of mature or middle-aged people and the elderly. Further suppose that the result of the comparison is that we discover a deep difference in the quality of the lives of the members of these two age groups, a difference that profoundly favors the younger one.

Many writers would be quick to point out that we will not find such a general inequality when we compare the elderly—meaning those who are 65 or older—to other age groups, assuming that the comparison is made in contemporary North America or Western Europe. Whatever might have been true in the past, the elderly now have lives that are not significantly worse than the lives of younger people. For example, in the United States the rate of poverty among the elderly is not measurably higher than the rate of poverty in the general population, and this has been so for many years.

Nevertheless, there is inequality when the comparison is confined to specific categories among the elderly. The lives of the people called the "old old"—people 75 and older (some writers reserve the term for those 85 years and older)—are on average significantly worse than the lives of younger people. The same is true of elderly women who never married or who married and subsequently divorced or were widowed.

To make the case vivid, imagine that the same city block contains a condominium complex and a retirement home. The residents of the complex are middle aged, middle class, affluent, and happy. The retirement home is old, overcrowded, and badly managed. Its residents receive adequate medical care, but their situation offers them little dignity and little opportunity for anything approaching happiness.

The case exhibits an extreme inequality, and even those who are not in general sympathetic to so-called "egalitarian" values might initially worry that it raises an issue of justice. Is it fair that some should live so well while their neighbors live so miserably?

Of course this inequality is not simply the result of social policies and institutions such as the nursing home. Many of the problems of the elderly—physical and mental frailty, poor health, declining powers, and even boredom, sadness, and loneliness—are at least in part the natural effects of aging. However, most of us think that natural inequality can call for some remedy, or for giving a special importance to helping those who are worst off under the inequality. Consider those born with severe mental and physical handicaps. We feel obligated to offer them special and sometimes expensive help, although their problems are caused by nature and not society.

The inequality between the young and the old that I have described can be especially troubling because it seems in some respects analogous to, for example, racial inequality. Some people live much worse lives than others, and they can be readily identified by some property other than that of being badly off— the inequality is rooted in age or race. In each case, this is a factor that the people in question are not responsible for. We cannot blame people for growing old and experiencing the problems that I have described or complain that they should have arranged for their lives to end in some more elegant way.

However, there is an obviously important difference between age inequality and racial inequality. African Americans will never become Caucasians, or vice versa, but the young do become old, and the old were once young. So we can suppose that the residents of the condominium complex will finish their lives in circumstances like those of the nursing home and that the people in the home used to be just as happy and affluent as their neighbors now are.

When we think about the past and the future as well as the present—that is, when we think about the complete lives of the people concerned instead of narrowly focusing on the current state of their lives—the inequality that was so troubling seems to vanish. The current inequality does not actually vanish, but it might seem to lose its importance, and we might lose our confidence that it raises a serious issue of justice.

As Norman Daniels has pointed out, the special case of treating people of different ages extremely unequally can be perfectly compatible with treating people equally.[2] At least people are treated equally in the sense that, when we consider their lives as temporal wholes, from birth to death, there might be no serious inequality between them. Why should we believe that the present unhappiness of the elderly is a concern of justice if those who are now young will experience similar unhappiness in their final years and if those who are now elderly were themselves happy in their youth?

It is tempting to draw an analogy to a medieval guild. The practitioners of a craft are divided into apprentices, journeymen, and master craftsmen. At any given moment, there are serious inequalities between the people who occupy the three different levels. But

2. "Because we age, treating people of different ages differently does not mean we are treating persons unequally. From the perspective of institutions that operate over a lifetime, unequal treatment of different age groups does not generate inequalities among persons." Norman Daniels, *Am I My Parents' Keeper?* (Oxford: Oxford University Press, 1988, 42).

suppose (unrealistically in the case of actual guilds) that everyone progresses through each of the three stages. Every apprentice perseveres and becomes a master craftsman. The hierarchical organization of the craft benefits everyone in the long run, considering their professional careers as wholes. Everyone is better off because of the guild system than if there were free competition among workers of different levels of experience and ability. Is there any reason to complain about the temporary inequalities among those people who are at different stages in their careers?

The example presents us with a puzzle, and perhaps a distinctively philosophical puzzle. On the one hand, at least for most of us, the initial question about justice is real and pressing. Yet when we think about the same case in a different way, the issue of justice seems to disappear. But this second look—at least this is my own experience—does not completely convince us that there is no reason to ask the fortunate young to help the distressed elderly. There at least seems to be an objection to allowing the elderly to live in those conditions, even if this treatment is maintained consistently over time so that eventually everyone suffers from it. Our complex reaction to the example shows us that we are uncertain how to think about fairness among people of different age groups.

One decisive response to the puzzle judges the example solely on the basis of the genuine equality among complete lives, asserting that the radical present inequality between the young and the old does not raise an issue of justice, although we might understandably be tempted to think that it does. According to this view, the appropriate temporal unit for the application of principles of justice are lifetimes, not temporal stages in lives or related to how individuals are faring at particular times during their lives.

Most moral philosophers who write about justice seem to adopt this view. A comment by Thomas Nagel is typical: "Remember that the subject of an egalitarian principle is not the distribution of particular rewards to individuals at some time, but the prospective quality of their lives as a whole, from birth to death."[3] Nagel is explicitly discussing egalitarian principles that treat equality as an important value. But writers who are not egalitarians make similar claims about the natural way of applying their distributive principles.[4] Since much of my discussion will be concerned with egalitarian views of justice, I will call this view complete lives egalitarianism.

The view can be supported by many arguments. The elderly are much worse off than their neighbors, but they were precisely that well off themselves when they were young, and their neighbors will experience equal misery when they are old. So it seems that their present hardship is fully compensated for by benefits that they enjoyed at some other stage of their lives. If the hardship is compensated for, how can it ground a claim of justice that they should be helped now, at the expense of their neighbors? Given the terms of the example, if there were to be a transfer of resources from the young to the old in the present, then the young people who made the sacrifice would never be compensated for it, so their complete lives would turn out to be somewhat worse than the lifetimes of the people who are now living in the retirement home.

However, we should realize how strong the implications of Nagel's view are. He states that justice is not concerned with

---

3. Thomas Nagel, *Equality and Partiality* (New York: Oxford University Press, 1991, 69).
4. One example is W. D. Ross. He believes that an individual's well-being should be proportional to his degree of virtue but thinks the proportion should hold between the total amount of well-being in the person's complete life and the total amount of virtue in the complete life: "What we perceive to be good is a condition of things in which the total pleasure enjoyed by each person in his life as a whole is proportional to his virtue similarly taken as a whole" (*The Right and the Good*, Oxford: Clarendon Press, 1930, 58).

distributing benefits and harms to people at particular times. Justice, thus, has no relation to synchronic distribution among people of different ages. To be more accurate, justice can only dictate that resources should be synchronically distributed among age groups in the way that will best realize fairness among complete lifetimes, whatever fairness among complete lifetimes might turn out to be. So Nagel is committed to a definite verdict about my example. The current inequality between the young and the old is not objectionable.

Nagel would be committed to the same conclusion about even more extreme cases. In her book *Old Age*, Simone de Beauvoir says that, in France in the 1960's, the elderly were "condemned to poverty, decrepitude, wretchedness, and despair" (p. 2), and regarded not as human beings but as "so many walking corpses" (p. 6)[5]. This seems to be a highly exaggerated picture of the lives of elderly people during that decade, and it certainly no longer fits the facts even if we were willing to grant that it once did. However, suppose it were accurate. Would there really be no unfairness in the members of the other age groups treating the old in that way, provided that everyone lived long enough to eventually be neglected and ignored in their turn, so that there were no differences among lifetimes?

These consequences of Nagel's view are intuitively troubling, even if we are not sure how to answer his arguments. I would make the stronger claim that the example makes it implausible to suppose that the lifetime perspective captures every consideration relevant to justice. This is not to say that we should not take up the lifetime perspective and compare the complete lives of different people. Still, the lifetime perspective is not the only way in which

---

5. Simone de Beauvoir, *Old Age* (London: Andre Deutsch and Weidenfeld and Nicolson, 1972, 2, 6).

we should think and it does not incorporate and give the proper degree of importance to every reason that is relevant for justice. Of course I cannot expect this claim to be simply granted, and I will be returning to this issue in the later chapters of this book.

I think that the ideas raised by the puzzle are also responsible for one frequently expressed attitude about the distribution of resources between the young and the old. This response comes from those who place great importance on the fact that things can even out over time when the different age groups experience lives of very different quality.

Everyone would agree that the questions about social security and health care that I have raised are serious practical problems. Initially it also seems that responses to them that change the relevant institutions will inevitably help some people and harm others. For example, in the case of medicine, we might decide to tax younger people at an even higher rate to support health care for the increasing numbers of the elderly, or alternatively decide to ration the provision of certain kinds of health care to the elderly. Both choices seem to have obvious advantages and disadvantages, and seem to create winners and losers.

Nevertheless, without denying these facts some feel that these choices do not involve a deep issue of interpersonal justice in the way that choices between genders, or races, or social classes do. Their claim is that we are not forced to choose among the claims of different people, satisfying the claims of some while allowing the claims of others to remain unmet.

This attitude is shared by those who manage the relevant institutions and by writers who are struggling to understand the moral implications of the transfers between generations. Robert Ball, a long-time administrator in the American social security program, assured Congress in 1975 "income security after retirement is not a matter of one group—those of working age—helping another group—the retired. It is a matter of everyone planning for a continuing income during the latter years of life."[6]

Ball's comment is remarkably similar to the ideas of Norman Daniels, who is responsible for the only fully worked-out philosophical theory of justice between age groups. Daniels tells his readers, "We must not look at the problem as one of justice between distinct groups in competition with each other, for example, between working adults who pay high premiums and the frail elderly who consume so many services. Rather, we must see that each group represents a stage of our lives. We must view the prudent allocation of resources through the stages of life as our guide to justice between groups."[7]

Ball and Daniels are suggesting that it is a mistake to think about these issues as presenting us with a clear conflict of interpersonal justice. Instead, we should consider the parallel between the two social groups of the young and the elderly and the two temporal stages of youth and old age inside a single person's life. Given this parallel, we should suppose that the best—and fairest—way of dividing resources between the two age -groups is just the same as the best way of dividing resources between the stages of youth and old age inside a person's life. Our problem can be understood as being concerned with dividing resources among different temporal stages inside one person's life, not with dividing resources among different lives. If these ideas are acceptable, the apparently interpersonal choice between young people and old people is equivalent to, or reduces to, a choice between the stages of youth and old age inside one life.

6. The source of the quote is Martha Derthick, *Policymaking For Social Security* (Washington, DC: The Brookings Institution, 1979, 253).
7. Daniels, 45.

Ball and Daniels think we should welcome their view as good news. In one sense, it is clear why. Suppose that, in the end, we reluctantly decide that our best choice is not to continue to demand high premiums from working adults to provide the many services for the elderly in need of them. If the authors are right we can at least think that we are not making the brute moral decision that the claims of the elderly are outweighed by those of younger people. The issues we are considering are not ones that divide us into competing groups with conflicting interests. They are ones that arise inside each of our lives, and that we should think about them in this way in order to resolve them and reach agreement about them.

Ball and Daniels count as optimists in another way. They believe that once we take the crucial step of conceiving the nature of the problem in their way, then at least the general outline of the right solution is obvious and uncontroversial. Designing the social security system becomes a matter of applying to a social institution the model of one person planning ahead for his retirement (Ball), and, in general, the distribution of resources among age groups should be determined by what is usually called prudential thinking about a single life (Daniels). Applying prudence to the general question of distributing resources throughout an entire lifetime is a difficult challenge, and it may turn out to involve theoretical problems as well as problems of detail, but it is not as contentious as weighing the moral claims of different people against one another and then choosing between them. It is important to emphasize another consequence of Ball's and Daniels's approach. When we consider our own futures, we do not ordinarily think in terms of justice (assuming that my choices about my own life will not harm other people). If I plan to work until I am 65 in order to build up my savings rather than retiring earlier, I do not wonder whether this choice is unfair to me between the ages of 60 and 65. Instead, I think about what will make my temporally complete life best on the whole. So I will not think in terms of the values that are usually associated with justice when we are considering conflicts among the interests of different people. Equality is one example of such a value. According to Ball and Daniels, such values will not be directly part of the answer to the question of the fairest distribution of resources among age groups.

Unlike Nagel's exclusive concern with complete lives, the view shared by Ball and Daniels (and by many other writers who discuss the distribution of health care and medical resources among age groups) can agree that there are constraints of justice that are intrinsically concerned with the temporal parts of lives. If the distribution between the condominium residents and the people in the nursing home does not match what a rational, prudent individual would chose for his own life, Daniels's view can condemn it as an injustice, not merely an inefficient way of dividing resources, despite the flawless equality between lifetimes that it generates. Nevertheless, that view derives these distributional constraints by thinking prudentially about a single life—in other words, by assuming the lifetime perspective in a distinctive way. So it might seem that the view has the extra advantage of respecting Nagel's reasons for thinking that the lifetime perspective is dominant.

1.3 MY POSITIVE VIEW

I will oppose the attitude that Ball and Daniels share. This is partly because I think that their positive view based on prudence gives the wrong answers to many of the specific questions that we will be considering. More fundamentally, I want to preserve the idea that the issues about generations and age groups involve genuine and deep problems of interpersonal justice, although they may resist the kind of thinking that philosophical theories of justice have traditionally employed. There are real conflicts between the claims of the young and the old, and the conflicts are neither transcended nor plausibly resolved by considering a single life and invoking prudential rationality. This view can be maintained without denying that we all age and live through the characteristic temporal stages of life, even if we suppose that consistency in the treatment of age -groups means that there are no important differences in the quality of peoples' complete lives.

With respect to assessing the institutions I have mentioned, my positive view will not be a narrow account of when people are being treated fairly by those institutions. One might suppose that, in the case of social security, this would simply be a matter of different generations and different individuals being roughly equal when we take into account both the contributions they make to the institution and the benefits they receive from it. Instead, my view is intended to express more general claims of justice that people possess to a certain level of welfare or well-being. These institutions, and perhaps also individual agents, will be constrained to attempt to meet these claims. The history of social security shows an attempt to respond to such a broader and more fundamental goal.

The principles of justice that my positive view applies to temporal parts of lives will be egalitarian, at least in a broad sense of the term. I will not attempt to make a general argument that egalitarianism must be at least one component of the best theory of morality. this does not mean that I will be merely assuming that egalitarianism is correct. The questions about distribution between the young and the old discussed will offer at least intuitive support for egalitarianism. A distinctively egalitarian concern can be recognized as one of the reasons that people have for supporting an institution such as social security.

The crucial feature of the view is that it applies egalitarian considerations to temporal parts of lives or to people at particular times. People can possess a claim of justice for a certain temporal stage of their lives, a claim that is independent of how they fare in terms of their lifetime as a whole. I grant that we also need to apply the egalitarian values at the level of complete lifetimes, but I think that a view that exclusively uses complete lives as the relevant temporal unit will be incomplete and unable to account for some of our strongest judgments.

It will be helpful to add an explanation of my terminology. When I speak of principles of justice for age groups, or justice between the young and the old, I am referring to principles that deal with distribution among the temporal parts of different lives and so constrain synchronic distribution among people of different age groups. Of course these principles of justice are not the only ones that apply to the individuals who belong to the age groups. There are also principles of justice concerned with complete lifetimes that need to be taken into account in deciding how to treat the members of different age groups and in designing such institutions as social security and the health care system. These principles could be included in an account of justice between the young and the old in a broader sense. However, I will call them principles of justice for generations, as opposed to principles of justice for age groups.

This choice involves terminological legislation on my part. It is helpful because it emphasizes the special nature of the principles concerned with temporal parts of lives, and because I think these principles are precisely what is at issue with many difficult questions about justice between the young and the old. But the terminology also involves a substantive moral claim, because many would reject these principles. There are principles that deserve to be called "principles of justice for age groups," and that are established distinct from principles concerned with complete lives.

Chapter 2 considers the arguments for why egalitarian moral concerns should include the temporal scope of a complete life. The arguments are individually and collectively persuasive, and a view that attempts to apply egalitarian principles to temporal parts of lives must respond to them. This chapter will only state and explain the arguments, not try to answer them. The answers will come later in chapters 4 and 5, which present my view of justice between age groups.

Chapter 3 deals with the view that identifies fairness among temporal parts of different lives with the distribution that would be chosen by prudence over the different temporal parts of one life. This idea is at the heart of Daniels's theory of justice between age groups, the prudential lifespan account. If, however, we decide to apply egalitarian principles to temporal parts of lives, it should not take this form. My criticisms of the prudential lifespan account will include both intuitive judgments about the consequences that I think the theory would lead to, and more theoretical objections that question the basic ideas in the theory.

Chapters 4 and 5 explain and defend my view on how to apply principles of justice to individual parts of lives. Rather than appealing to prudential thinking, this view is concerned with the egalitarian values of equality and priority. Chapter 4 discusses the application of equality to temporal parts of lives, and Chapter 5 discusses priority. In the case of both values, I show how the arguments for complete lives egalitarianism can be answered. I also determine the most plausible ways of applying these values to temporal parts of lives. The two chapters also have another goal. If we apply an egalitarian value to parts of lives, it should be priority not equality. My arguments will be focused on the application to temporal parts of lives, not general arguments that priority is more defensible than equality.

Chapter 6 considers some further questions about the views defended in chapters 4 and 5, arguing that applying principles of justice to temporal parts of lives does not depend on any particular theory of the nature of personal identity. For example, applying such principles does not depend on awarding a special ontological status to temporal parts of lives, or thinking that a person consists of a series of related selves. Chapter 6 will also argue that the application does not depend on there being a significant amount of psychological change over the lifetime of the person. The chapter also discusses the relationship between egalitarian priority and prudence and it defends an implication of my positive view that we make priority judgments both inside lives and across different lives with the same degree of strength.

Chapter 7 discusses a new question about prudential thinking. When we make a decision that will importantly affect our lives in the future, we may realize that our current goals and values are significantly different from the goals and values that we will hold at the future time when the decision will impact our lives. How should we decide what to do? Should we decide on the strength of our present values or instead use our predicted future values; or should we give weight to both sets of values? This is a puzzle for prudential rationality, one thought to involve deep issues concerning the significance of time for rationality and the importance of the distinction between past, present, and future. The chapter suggests a response to the puzzle.

Chapter 8 considers an important issue for the elderly, the condition and treatment of people with Alzheimer's disease and other forms of dementia. It assesses the philosophical debate over the degree of autonomy possessed by these patients and the nature of the interests that they possess and the kinds of goods they are capable of experiencing.

Chapter 9 draws some conclusions about the policies of the institutions that are centrally concerned with transfers between age groups. It also answers the concern expressed by some writers that we cannot properly understand justice among age groups and generations because they are amorphous entities and there are no clear criteria for individuating them.

Chapter 2

Complete Lives Egalitarianism

2.1 THE TEMPORAL SCOPE OF EQUALITY

Since this chapter is concerned with a particular kind of egalitarianism, I should begin by identifying some related issues that I will not be able to properly consider. I will assume that egalitarianism is ultimately concerned with well-being and not with opportunity, resources, or capabilities. Egalitarian values should be concerned with what is most important, and well-being is more important than the other items cited. I will make this assumption when I am discussing equality between complete lives, equality between temporal parts of lives (chapter 4), and when I am discussing the egalitarian notion of priority (chapter 5). This is a controversial view, but I am not in a position to argue for it. However, I will try as best as I can to stay neutral among different accounts of the nature of well-being. I think some theories of well-being are much more plausible than others, but I hope the conclusions I draw will be persuasive whether well-being is explained in terms of utility, pleasure and pain, an agent's evaluative judgments about his own life, or perfectionist goods. Of course I may be mistaken, and it is possible that some of my claims about equality and priority are only plausible if we hold a particular view about the nature of well-being.

Suppose, when we consider the example presented in chapter 1, we think the best choice is to help the people in the nursing home. The example serves two purposes. First, it shows that we are inclined to make at least some egalitarian judgments about the issues I am discussing. We are choosing to help the people in the nursing home despite the fact that we could help others more; that is an egalitarian choice. We should expect the decision to be based on some egalitarian value, perhaps the value of equality, priority, or sufficiency. This seems to show that egalitarian values play some role in understanding justice between the young and the old.

Second, the example seems to show that those egalitarian values will not always apply to the temporal scope of a complete life because we choose to help the older person even though it creates inequality that otherwise would not exist between his complete lifetime and the complete life of a younger person. So to explain the judgment we must apply an egalitarian value with a temporal scope that is less than a complete lifetime.

However, we should not immediately draw these conclusions on the strength of the example. In particular, we need to consider the view that if justice between the young and the old includes egalitarian values, they should be exclusively concerned with complete lifetimes.

Philosophical theories of justice tend to assign their distributive principles the temporal scope of a lifetime. People are thus being treated fairly if the principles are satisfied when we compare one person's life considered as a whole with another person's life also considered as a whole.

There are several reasons why this is so. Sometimes the choice of a lifetime as the appropriate temporal scope depends on specific features of particular theories about justice. For example, contractualists believe that the correct principles of justice are those that people would collectively agree on in a free choice of principles made under specified conditions. They usually include the thought (explicitly or implicitly) that the choice should be made with a view to the quality of the complete lives that people could expect to live if they were governed by those principles. One reason for structuring the choice in this way is that it is intended to lead to principles that will govern social institutions that influence our lives in important ways from their beginning to their end. Given that aim for the theory of justice, the resulting principles should require that we compare the quality of people's lifetimes.

2.2 THE ARGUMENTS FOR COMPLETE LIVES EGALITARIANISM

However, there are also deeper and more general reasons for choosing lifetimes as the temporal unit. I will explain these reasons with reference to an egalitarian theory of justice, though the reasons might have parallels in the case of nonegalitarian theories.

The first reason is the concern about compensation emphasized by Nagel. A deep inequality between two people at a particular time is compatible with their complete lifetimes being equal in the relevant respects. Suppose that we decide to apply an egalitarian principle to people at a particular time or a particular temporal stage of life. If we do this, then we might decide to remove the inequality inside that temporal unit by redistributing resources from the better-off person to the worse-off person. However, then we are ignoring the benefits that the worse-off person must have received at some other time if his complete life is equal to the complete life of the better-off person. It is a mistake to ignore those benefits: They are morally important and compensate the person for the inequality experienced at the particular time we began by considering.

Many people think that it is a fundamental truth for morality and rationality that inside one life, a benefit at one time can compensate for a harm experienced at another. Since the person's disadvantage at the time of the inequality is compensated for at some other time, it is unfair rather than fair to give him an extra advantage by eliminating that inequality. In order to avoid this kind of overcompensation, we should focus on complete lifetimes and only redistribute when it will remove an inequality between complete lives. I call this reason for only applying the egalitarian principle to lifetimes the argument from compensation.

This reason has a special connection with egalitarian theories of justice. Egalitarianism came into its own as a moral theory during the 1970s. The most important factor was the publication of John Rawls's *Theory of Justice*, but Ronald Dworkin, Thomas Scanlon, and Nagel also made valuable contributions.[1] These writers produced egalitarian moral theories that sometimes differed significantly in their content. Apart from the differences, the writers tended to share certain ideas about the source or the starting point of egalitarianism. At least at the deepest level, they tended to say the same things about egalitarian distributional constraints.

1. John Rawls, *A Theory of Justice* (Cambridge, MA: Harvard University Press, 1971); Ronald Dworkin, "Justice and Rights" in *Taking Rights Seriously* (Cambridge, MA: Harvard University Press, 1977, 150–83); Thomas Nagel, *The Possibility of Altruism* (Oxford UK: Clarendon Press, 1970) and "Equality" in *Mortal Questions* (Cambridge UK: Cambridge University Press, 1979, 106–27); and Thomas Scanlon, "Nozick on Rights, Liberty, and Property" in *Philosophy & Public Affairs* 6, no. 1,1976, 3–25; and "Contractualism and Utilitarianism" in *Utilitarianism and Beyond*, Amartya Sen and Bernard Williams, eds. (Cambridge UK: Cambridge University Press, 1982, 103–28).

One shared idea was that egalitarianism involves, and perhaps depends on, there being a fundamental difference between interpersonal and intrapersonal judgments. Interpersonal judgments distribute benefits and harms among different people and so across different lives. Intrapersonal judgments distribute benefits and harms inside one life, a life led by a single self-identical person.

Intrapersonal judgments, the authors held, are governed by a maximizing principle. In the case of a single person, we need only be concerned with achieving the greatest possible surplus of benefits over harms, irrespective of how those benefits and harms would be distributed inside the person's life from its beginning to its end. Prudential rationality on the part of the person whose life it is, and benevolent moral concern on the part of someone acting in that person's best interest, are complementary in pursuing this goal.

By contrast, interpersonal judgments are not governed by a maximizing principle. We should not simply aim at bringing about the greatest possible surplus of benefits over harms when they will be experienced by different people. Just because we are dealing with different lives, distributional constraints apply, expressed by the egalitarian principle, which might be interpreted in different ways and assigned different degrees of strength when it is weighed against other moral values.

The writers tended to give the same explanation of this shared thought, claiming that, if a benefit and harm occur in the same life and the benefit is greater than the harm, then the benefit morally outweighs the harm. It is better for the person to experience both than to experience neither. However, if the harm and benefit will be experienced by different people, the larger benefit might not morally outweigh the lesser harm. It is not necessarily better for one person to experience the harm and the other person to experience the benefit than for neither person to be benefited or harmed. The writers suggest that it is the moral importance of the so-called separateness of persons that can prevent the benefit from outweighing the harm.[2] In the interpersonal case, the two individuals are separate persons with separate lives, while in the intrapersonal case there is only a single person and one life, so there is nothing to prevent the benefit from outweighing the harm.[3]

I will call these ideas the standard egalitarian view, and offering them as an explanation of an egalitarian moral concern has certain consequences. In particular, the price of defending the existence of egalitarian distributional constraints between lives is conceding that there are no such distributional constraints inside lives. This is a price that the egalitarian writers of the 1970s were not at all reluctant to pay. In addition—although people did not remark on this consequence at the time—the standard egalitarian view restricts the application of egalitarian principles to peoples'

2. Some egalitarians believed that the separateness of persons led initially to a moral position that was distinct from the egalitarian distributive principle itself, for example, the view that benefits or harms in one life could never morally outweigh benefits or harms in a different life. They suggested that the egalitarian distributive principle could be derived from this moral position, which supposes that moral importance of the separateness of persons can be used as a premise in an argument for the value of equality. For criticisms of such an argument, see David Brink "The Separateness of Persons, Distributive Norms, and Moral Theory" in *Value, Welfare, and Morality*, R.G Frey and Christopher W. Morris, eds. (Cambridge: Cambridge University Press, 1993, 252–89); and my "Egalitarianism and the Separateness of Persons" in *Canadian Journal of Philosophy* 18 (1988) 205–25.

3. Thomas Nagel comments that the fact that benefits can outweigh harms inside a life does not by itself give us a reason to think that benefits do not outweigh harms across lives—that is, maximizing in intrapersonal cases does not positively support accepting egalitarianism in interpersonal cases (Nagel "Equality," 120). I agree. The contrast between intrapersonal and interpersonal judgments is central to egalitarianism because, once we have agreed that intrapersonal judgments are governed by a maximizing principle, we must think that interpersonal judgments are fundamentally different from intrapersonal judgments if we are to be egalitarians.

complete lifetimes. The concern for equality will turn out to be a concern for equality among peoples' complete lives.

This is shown by the argument from compensation. Can inequality between two simultaneous temporal parts in two different lives by itself generate a reason for trying to create equality between the two temporal parts? We are supposing that benefits can outweigh harms over time inside lives if not across lives. So to decide whether to remove the simultaneous inequality, we must scrutinize the rest of the two lives to find out whether outweighing and compensation are present. In the end, we have to compare the complete lives of the two people before we can decide whether to make the interpersonal judgment to redistribute between them. As a result, the concern for equality is a concern that their complete lives should be equally good. If the standard egalitarian view is correct, the restriction to complete lives follows from the foundations of egalitarianism.

A second argument for the focus on lifetimes is based on prudential rationality. It is almost uncontroversial that prudential rationality is ultimately concerned with complete lifetimes. The goal of prudence is to make one's life as a whole as good as it can possibly be. For example, suppose someone were to decide to make his life better when he was young at the cost of making his life worse when he was old. Further, suppose the well-being that he would gain during his youth was significantly exceeded by the well-being he would lose when he was old. His life as a whole would be made worse by this choice. The choice could be described as making a particular temporal part of his life better at the cost of making his lifetime worse. This choice would also seem to be irrational. We would draw the same conclusion if a person were to do the same thing in promoting the welfare of another person, which shows that promoting one's well-being at a particular time or during a particular temporal stage of life is not a goal that can compete against that of making one's life as a whole as good as it can be. The ultimate goal of prudence is the quality of a lifetime.

Some would argue that, if prudence is ultimately concerned with lifetimes, the same should be true of moral thinking. We should not give intrinsic importance to applying a principle of justice to a temporal unit that is less than a complete lifetime. In the case of egalitarian principles, we should not give intrinsic importance to inequality at a particular time, unless that inequality is not compensated for so that the result is inequality between lifetimes.

This claim might not be convincing on its own, but it can be strengthened by an additional point about prudence. A distribution that involves considerable inequality between people at particular times would possibly achieve both equality among people's lifetimes and benefit all of those people more than any other distribution. If we were to apply an egalitarian principle of justice to people at particular times, we might be tempted to object to this distribution, but this objection seems unreasonable. If we insist on removing the inequality at particular times, we will make everyone worse off. Assuming that the people in question are prudentially rational, they would unanimously choose the first distribution, so how can it be regarded as a worse outcome? They seem to have a good reason for choosing it— the alternative distribution would make each of them worse off, and it would not have compensating benefits for anyone. I call this reason for focusing on complete lives the argument from prudence.

There is a third reason for the restriction to lifetimes that is as powerful as the others but harder to state. Almost all of us believe that a human lifetime is a morally important unit. For example, we have already considered the egalitarian view that, although a benefit can compensate for harm inside a life, it is not clear that benefits can morally compensate for harms across lives. If we agree, we are assigning a certain kind of moral importance to the difference between different lives and so giving moral significance to the boundary that surrounds a single life.

We should treat a single lifetime as a morally important unit, though it is not easy to say exactly what kind of moral significance a lifetime has. It is also difficult to give a deeper explanation of what this significance depends on. Presumably it is connected to what could be loosely called the unity of the life lived by the person, but it is not clear how this connection should be developed and what kind of unity is in question. Still, despite the vagueness, we can point to some implications for morality and for egalitarianism, in particular.

To return to the example given in chapter 1, when we compare the current life of a resident of the nursing home with the current life of the resident of condominium complex we might feel that fairness compels us to help the elderly person. But we are comparing a temporal part of one life to a temporal part of a different life and using the comparison to draw a conclusion about how to treat those two people. Our comparison cuts across the boundaries between different lives. This is not surprising, since the value of equality is standardly applied to different people. But we have to be sure that we are entitled to draw the conclusion that we are tempted to make. The complex object of our comparison, a temporal part of one life compared to a temporal part of a different life, does not share the unity of a single life. So it is not clear what kind of moral importance the comparison possesses. We are also drawing the conclusion without taking into account the past youth of the elderly person or the future old age of the condominium dweller.

The old age and the youth of the person who is now old are different temporal parts of the same life, and they are each a morally significant unit. The connections between that person's youth and old age, however they might be understood, are clearly stronger than the connections between that person's old age and the youth of a different person.

This observation points to the conclusion that we should connect or combine the stages of youth and old age in a single life before we compare either of these temporal stages with a temporal stage in some other life. When we combine the two stages, we find that the first stage contained great happiness and the second great misery. When we consider the life of the person who is now young and respect the moral importance of that person's life, we find the same thing, a stage of great happiness and a stage of great misery. So there seems to be no room for a complaint about fairness on the part of either person. A complaint exists only if we compare the youth of one person to the old age of the other person before we have connected them to the other temporal stages of the lives of which they are part. But doing this seems to violate the moral importance of the unity of a single life and the moral significance of the difference between separate, individual lives. We must view a temporal stage of a particular life in the context of the life of which it is a part before we award that person a claim of justice against others. Doing this is once again making claims about justice depend on complete lives, not on temporal parts of lives.

The final argument arises from an issue that has dominated recent discussions of egalitarianism. Many egalitarians have struggled to give notions of choice and responsibility (and even desert) a significant role to play in their theories. Instead of simply saying that inequality is bad (or unjust), they suggest that inequality might not be bad, or might be less bad, if it has resulted from the choices of the people who are worse off under the inequality, or if they are in certain ways responsible for the condition of their lives.

Egalitarian views of this sort can take many different forms, and there are complicated debates about which versions are the most plausible. But most of the views at least hold that a choice made by a person at one time can be morally important in deciding how it is fair to treat that person at some other time. In the case of the example in chapter 1, perhaps some of the residents of the nursing home are badly off now because of imprudent choices that they made earlier in their lives. In that case, these egalitarians might say that their responsibility is relevant to the question of whether the present inequality counts as an injustice and should be addressed. So it seems that, to give the proper weight to facts about choice and responsibility, we must be prepared in principle to consider the past and the future when assessing a present inequality. This consideration might make it seem natural to choose complete lifetimes as the relevant temporal unit when we are applying egalitarian principles. Giving our principles broad temporal scope allows us to include the facts about choice and responsibility that are relevant to determining the moral importance of the inequalities that we are considering. I call this argument the argument from responsibility.

Collectively these arguments seem very powerful. Some would say that, even if we are inclined to think there is injustice of some sort in the case of the nursing home and the condominiums, we should pull ourselves back from that conclusion. An intuitive judgment carries some weight, but we should be prepared to abandon it in the light of strong arguments. Perhaps the intuitive judgment can be explained away as emotional sympathy or as the result of giving the egalitarian principle a narrow temporal scope when reflective thought would show us that this was unjustified.

Nevertheless, I will argue that we should apply egalitarian values to temporal units other than complete lifetimes and that we should reject complete lives egalitarianism. I think that we should apply egalitarian values to lifetimes, but I contend that the application to stages in lives is also legitimate. In my view, this application is the heart of justice between the young and the old. I will use intuitive judgments about particular cases to motivate and to construct my positive account of justice between age groups, but it is also necessary to reply to the arguments for the complete lives view, a response I provide in subsequent chapters.

Chapter 3

The Prudential Lifespan Account

3.1 DANIELS'S VIEW

Suppose that we are not convinced by complete lives egalitarianism. We suspect that there is a distinctive issue of justice between age groups, a kind of justice that applies its principles to temporal parts of lives. We have seen that familiar theories of justice will be of little help in understanding this kind of fairness, because those theories deal with lifetimes.

That is why I will begin with Daniels's view. He agrees that there is a distinctive kind of justice concerned with age groups that constrains how resources are synchronically distributed among people of different ages. If he is right, unfairness in distribution between the young and the old can exist, an unfairness distinct from that involved when different generations are treated unequally over their lifetimes. For Daniels, the principles of justice between age groups are different from the principles for complete lives. His theory recognizes reasons of justice that are concerned with temporal parts of individuals' lives. The reasons are claims to be treated in a certain way during a temporal part of a life.

However, Daniels does not abandon the focus on complete lives. His central idea is that we can discover the best way of synchronically distributing resources among people of different ages by thinking prudentially about a diachronic distribution across the different temporal stages of a single complete lifetime. Prudence shows us what justice requires between young and the old. The fair distribution between the young and the old is the distribution that would be chosen by a prudential individual allocating resources to the temporal stages in her own life. The goal of prudential rationality in choosing a distribution is to make the life viewed as a temporal whole as good as it can possibly be. So in the case of this kind of justice, prudence and justice turn out to coincide.

There is such a distinctive kind of justice, but Daniels's theory gives the wrong account of its source and its content. He offers a complex, rather than simple, version of the lifetime perspective. Unlike Nagel, he does not suppose that justice is only concerned with lifetimes and imposes no intrinsic constraints on distribution at particular times. Consequently, he can say that there is unfairness between age groups even when there is no unfairness in terms of complete lives. The principles of justice for lifetimes might be satisfied, but the distribution among people of different ages might not be the one prudence would choose. Daniels would say that this distribution was inefficient, since peoples' lives would be better if the prudential distribution were implemented instead. But he would also count it as an injustice that can only be appreciated by thinking in terms of distribution among temporal parts of lives.

Daniels believes that distributional constraints apply both to lifetimes and to temporal stages of lives, but he proposes that we understand the constraints applying to stages in lives by first thinking about complete lives. We discover the fair synchronic distribution between people of different ages by imagining that the simultaneous temporal stages of different lives are the non-simultaneous temporal stages in a single life, and by asking what distribution across those temporal stages would be best for that constructed life considered as a whole.

As a result, the concern with lifetimes dominates the concern with temporal parts of lives. If there is a conflict between the principles of justice for complete lives and the principles of justice for temporal parts of lives, the principles of justice for complete lives should win. Creating fairness between complete lives trumps achieving fairness between temporal parts of lives.

In Daniels's terminology, the principles dealing with lifetimes constitute the frame theory of justice. The prudential lifespan account, which comprises Daniels's theory about fairness between age groups, operates within that framework. Although Daniels does not explicitly commit himself to this claim, the frame theory should be egalitarian. The frame theory is responsible for creating fairness between complete lives, and then the prudential lifespan account creates justice in the distribution over temporal parts of lives.

Daniels's theory is reductionist in several ways. It supposes that a synchronic question—what would be a fair distribution of resources at a given time between people of different ages—reduces to a diachronic question—how should resources be distributed across the temporal stages of a life where those stages succeed one another in time. Second, his theory supposes that a question about temporal stages in lives—for example, how should resources be distributed between one person's old age and another person's middle years—reduces to a question about lifetimes. We answer the question about temporal stages by thinking about the distribution that would maximize the quality of a complete life. Third, Daniels supposes that an interpersonal question, how to divide resources between different people, reduces to an intrapersonal question, how should resources be divided between the different stages of one life. Fourth, the theory suggests that a question about justice, what is the fair distribution between people of different ages, reduces to a question about prudential thinking, what distribution of resources in a single life would maximize the overall quality of that life. The theory is reductionist in that it claims that the right answer to the second question in each pair of questions will provide the right answer to the first question in the pair.

Daniels seems to think that if the reduction of the interpersonal question to the intrapersonal question is acceptable and if the reduction of the question about temporal parts of lives to the question about lifetimes is also acceptable, this establishes the acceptability of the reduction of the issue of fairness to that of prudence.

Daniels realizes that people might be suspicious of the claimed equivalences, and he tries to remove their reservations:

> The lifespan account involves a fundamental shift of perspective. We must not look at the problem as one of justice between distinct groups in competition with each other, between working adults who pay high premiums and the frail elderly who consume so many services. Rather, we must see that each group represents a stage of our lives. We must view the prudent allocation of resources through the stages of life as our guide to justice between groups. The suggestion that we shift perspective may seem a conjurer's trick.... But this shift of perspective is no trick.... What we need is to see ourselves at other stages of our lives, benefiting from our own...prudent savings. (74)

The prudential lifespan account is a kind of trick, although of course the conjuring is well intentioned. There is a real issue of interpersonal justice about distribution between the young and the old. Different kinds of moral claims are relevant to the issue, and there are conflicts between the claims of different people that cannot be dissolved by changing perspective and imagining that the temporal parts of different lives belong to the same life. We may no longer be able to see these conflicts after the change of perspective because the new perspective is incomplete, not because the conflicting claims do not exist. We should resist the reductionism of the prudential lifespan account. Justice between the young and the old does not reduce to an intrapersonal question about prudential distribution inside an individual life.

In explaining the prudential lifespan account, Daniels stresses that the distribution that results will not create inequality among people, by which he means inequality among their complete lives. This is one of his reasons for thinking that the prudential lifespan account does not cross the boundaries between different lives. This feature of the prudential lifespan account supposedly makes it appropriate to choose a prudential distribution inside a single life.

But the theory cannot guarantee equality in terms of complete lives. People will live lives of different lengths, and because of this, some complete lives will be better or worse than others. To be fair, this problem would arise for any theory that deals with this subject. But we can ask how Daniels's view would attempt to cope with it. Since it is the frame theory that is concerned with fairness between complete lives, this theory would be responsible for minimizing inequality between lifetimes. It is strange that Daniels does not tell us more about the frame theory or more about the division of labor between the frame theory and the prudential lifespan account (the part of the theory concerned with distribution across temporal parts of lives). The frame theory must be egalitarian if it is to minimize inequality between complete lives. The prudential lifespan account proper does relatively little work with respect to achieving this goal. Consistently maintaining the prudential distribution over time would not in itself create inequality between complete lives. But any distribution over temporal parts of lives consistently maintained over time would have the same claim to not create inequality between lifetimes, including the distribution that prudence would be least likely to choose. So avoiding lifetime inequality, in this sense, is not a special merit of the prudential lifespan account and does not justify Daniels's claim that, when the prudential account distributes over the temporal stages in different lives, it is not crossing the boundaries between lives in a morally significant way. For these reasons Daniels does not establish that it is innocuous to treat the prudential distribution inside a single life as the principle of fairness for a distribution over the temporal parts of different lives.

However, my criticism of Daniels's theory is not based on the fact that it does permit some lifetime inequality. There are other serious objections to the view that would arise, even if all lives were the same length and even if there was no inequality between lifetimes.

Daniels's theory is just one example of a more general approach to fairness among age groups. I hope to give reasons for doubting the correctness of the approach itself, not just Daniels's version of it. The approach starts from a person thinking prudentially about his own life and uses this as the model for just distribution between the temporal parts of different lives.

Dworkin appeals to prudential reasoning to determine the fair distribution of medical resources among people of different ages.[1]

1. Ronald Dworkin, "Justice and the High Cost of Health" in *Sovereign Virtue* (Cambridge, MA: Harvard University Press, 2000, 307–19). Dworkin is only one of many writers to appeal to prudence in determining the fair way to allocate medical resources among people of different ages. Roughly the same idea is defended by Dan Brock in *Life and Death: Philosophical Essays in Biomedical Ethics* (Cambridge: Cambridge University

Dworkin calls his view the "prudent insurance ideal." It is intended to answer many questions apart from those concerned with age groups specifically, but Dworkin emphasizes the application of the view to the elderly.

He asks us to imagine that resources have been divided into fair lifetime shares for different people, according to whatever account of fairness we think is best (his own view is that lifetime shares should be equal, but he does not insist on this in applying the theory). So his view about medical care is framed by lifetime considerations in the way the prudential lifespan account is. Dworkin considers a person using his share of resources to buy insurance against possible harms, including health insurance that will determine the care and treatments that would be made available to him at different ages, if they are needed. The purchase is made in a competitive market. Since his resources are limited, he has to weigh health insurance against other goods and determine the content of the health insurance he will buy. His choice is based on prudence. He wants to make his life best overall, considering it as a temporal whole. Like Daniels, Dworkin claims that this hypothetical prudential choice shows us what is fair to provide to the elderly.

Dworkin does not precisely specify the choice that prudence would make or fully set out the reasoning that is supposed to lead to it. However, he does draw some controversial conclusions. He thinks that a prudent chooser would not buy insurance providing life-extending medical treatments if he became seriously ill at an advanced age and was also suffering from dementia. The cost of these treatments might be extreme, compared to custodial care in a nursing home without medical intervention to prolong his life. So the insurance that provided them would have a high premium.

Press, 1993, chapter 12). I focus on Dworkin because he uses the idea to draw challenging conclusions.

Dworkin thinks that, given the person's age and mental condition, having the insurance would add little to the quality of his life as a whole. It would be more prudent to insure against serious but non-life-threatening medical problems that might occur earlier in life. So Dworkin concludes that justice does not require us to provide life-extending treatment to elderly people who find themselves in that condition.

Richard Posner comments that Dworkin's conclusion is beyond the gravitational field of American morality.[2] We should not simply assume that the conclusion is morally vicious, but we might find it troubling. In chapter 5 I will explain a view about the fair distribution of health care that might justify a different conclusion.

Daniels draws some reasonably specific conclusions on the strength of his theory,[3] claiming that the prudential deliberator, thinking about income and other economic resources, would choose equality between maturity and old age. She would want to have roughly the same amount of resources at her disposal during those two stages of her life.

His conclusion does not seem objectionable, even if we might not be convinced that it is the right answer to the question of distribution between the elderly and the middle aged. However, I will argue that Daniels is wrong to think that his theory will lead

2. Posner's comment in *Aging and Old Age* (Chicago: University of Chicago Press, 1995, 256–57) is actually about Dan Brock who reaches a similar conclusion, but Posner links it to Dworkin, 267–68.

3. In assessing the prudential lifespan account, I depart in important ways from the theory as Daniels presents it. For Daniels, the theory is concerned with the distribution of opportunity, not well-being. One reason for this choice is that he wants to bring health care under a principle of equality of opportunity, rather than equality of welfare. He also believes that introducing well-being would mean taking into account peoples' values and views of the good, and he thinks it is important to remain neutral about these matters. I have altered the theory because I think that egalitarian principles are more persuasive if they focus on well-being. I think discussing the theory in Daniels's terms would not change my criticisms of the view.

to this result.[4] Someone deciding how to maximize the quality of her life as a whole would assign significantly fewer economic resources to the last stage of her life, especially when we consider extreme old age. When we see what the conclusions of the prudential lifespan account turn out to be, I think we will find them objectionable.

3.2 OBJECTIONS TO THE APPEAL TO PRUDENCE

Posner[5] and Tyler Cowen[6] also criticize the appeal to prudence, agreeing that the view will treat the elderly harshly. They assume that the prudential choice is made by a relatively young person who is aware of her own age. They claim that, as a result, the choice will be biased in favor of the interests of the young and might also reflect a tendency to care less about the distant future. We should not let the person's views and goals when she is young determine how she will be treated when she is old.

However, these criticisms misunderstand the nature of the choice that Daniels intends. He requires that the person should not know her age, precisely in order to avoid this kind of time bias. He also supposes that she does not know what her specific goals and values are, both now and in the future. So she will not

4. There is a difference between Daniels and Dworkin over the nature of the conclusions that the appeal to prudence will generate. Dworkin believes the results will be radical, at least in the case of scarce and expensive life-extending medical treatment. Daniels believes that the conclusions will be moderate and generous to the elderly. As my discussion of Daniels shows, I think the appeal to prudence would to lead to radical conclusions that would strictly limit the claims of the elderly.
5. Posner's criticism (266–67) is aimed at Dan Brock and Ronald Dworkin rather than Norman Daniels.
6. In "Comment on Daniels and McKerlie" in *Justice Across Generations* Lee M. Cohen ed. (Washington, DC: Public Policy Institute, American Association of Retired Persons, 1993, 227–36.

discount her old age because it is in the distant future, since for all she knows she is already old. She cannot favor her present projects if she does not know what they are. Arguably, the criticisms do apply to Dworkin who tells us that the representative agent making the choice is roughly 25 years old and apparently knows his age. Nothing in Dworkin's discussion suggests that the chooser does not know his current goals and values. These features of the choice compromise Dworkin's theory.

My criticisms of Daniels are aimed at showing that, even if the choice is made behind a veil of ignorance and even if it treats the different temporal stages of our lives impartially in the sense demanded by prudence, it will still permit intuitively objectionable inequality between the young and the old.

There are three different reasons for this conclusion. First, the chooser does not know how long her life will be. She is planning for a future that does not have a determined limit, although it will, in the end, be limited by her death. But she does not know when death will come, so she knows it is possible that she will not live long enough to use the resources that she might choose to save for old age. She does not know her age when she chooses, but she knows that it is significantly less likely that her own life will include extreme old age than that she will live to be 60.

Prudential rationality will take this consideration into account by discounting her potential welfare at the age of, for example, 95, by the likelihood that she will not actually live that long. This is a general reason for prudential rationality to favor the earlier stages of life in allocating resources. The force of the reason increases in strength as we consider more and more advanced ages.

Imagine that the chooser has a supply of safety deposit boxes and resources that can be placed in the boxes. Each box is labeled for a specific age. The rule governing the choice is that on the day of, for example, her eightieth birthday she opens the box labelled for that age, and she must live for the next year on the resources that the box contains. If she dies before reaching 80, she never uses the resources she put in that box or the resources in boxes assigned to even greater ages. Given these conditions, how much would a prudent person place in the box for the age of 100? Surely very little, but the prudential lifespan account stipulates that people who live into extreme old age only deserve that amount of resources.

It is fair to use this example against Daniels who sees the prudential choice as distributing a fixed amount of resources over a lifetime. However, the objection might be easier to answer if the prudential agent were instead deciding whether to buy insurance against extreme old age, as in Dworkin's theory. We would still discount our concern with the quality of our lives at the age of 100 by the unlikelihood of our living to be that old. But because few people reach that age, the premium for insurance against that eventuality might not be prohibitive. So prudence might dictate purchasing the insurance.

This consideration might lead us to prefer Dworkin's version of the appeal to prudence.[7] But Dworkin does not spell his view out in enough detail to show how prudence would reach the conclusions that he supports. If it were spelled out, it is possible that a weaker version of the first objection would still apply to it. The major problem for Dworkin's theory is that the prudential choice that he envisages is so wide ranging, it is difficult to draw any specific conclusions from it.

7. In answering my first criticism, Daniels suggests that perhaps the prudential choice should be understood as deciding whether or not to invest in an annuity that would guarantee the chooser support during his old age, irrespective of how long his life might last (Norman Daniels, "The Prudential Lifespan Account: Objections and Replies" in *Justice Across Generations*, 24). This change would bring Daniels's view close

There is another way for Daniels to answer the first objection. In recent work, he stipulates that the prudential chooser must assume that she will live through all of the temporal stages of a life, including extreme old age. This is a different version of the prudential choice than the one I have discussed, and it obviously escapes the first objection, since the concern about the length of life is ruled out.

This version of the prudential choice brings its own difficulties. Daniels wants to use the device of a prudential choice to determine the fair distribution of scarce life-extending medical resources. Applying prudence to this issue requires taking into account the likelihood of death at various ages. So he might be forced to claim that there are two different choices, one subject to the above restriction that reveals the fair way to distribute most resources, and one without the restriction that shows the fair way to distribute resources necessary to prolong life. If each choice is supposed to reveal something about fairness, why should there be such a significant difference in the conditions applied to the two choices?

My second objection does not depend on the unlikelihood of living to be very old. The prudential thinker will know that, in general, resources will make less of a contribution to her well-being if they are used during extreme old age rather than at some earlier stage. Since prudence is concerned with the quality of her life as a whole, she will assign many more resources to the part of her life when they can be used the most effectively.

---

to Dworkin's prudent insurance model, and it would blunt the force of the first objection. However, Daniels does not attempt to integrate the annuity proposal with the rest of his theory or to explain what conclusions this important change in the theory would lead to.

For most of us, the middle part of life will have the most influence on the success and failure of our lives. Suppose we must experience 30 consecutive years of success followed by 30 years of failure, but the temporal location of the two periods is up to us. Most of us would choose to succeed between the ages of 40 and 70 to fail between the ages of 70 and 100, and not the other way round.

Between the ages of 20 and, for example, 65, we try to achieve our most important goals, when our ability to achieve these goals is at its peak. We establish relationships, raise children, and do our best work in terms of a career. In old age, we add the final touches to what we have already done, reflect on the past, or turn to activities that we had set aside before because we had other priorities. If middle age matters most to the overall significance of a life, prudence will favor it in distributing resources. Of course some individuals are exceptions, and in their case old age defines their lives as a whole, but such cases are rare and the prudential choice does not address the exceptions.

The second objection to the prudential lifespan account is that the prudential choice will favor middle age and short-change the elderly in an unfair way. But it is not clear how powerful the objection is. It shows that prudence would distribute resources unequally over the different temporal stages of a life. However, it also provides a reason for the inequality. The goals that we pursue in the middle part of our lives are the most important for the value of our complete lives. We might think that, if the inequalities have this basis, there is no reason to consider them objectionable. Furthermore, the synchronic inequality between age groups that this factor would generate might not run very deep.

The third objection is related to the second, but it reveals a deeper problem for the appeal to prudence concerning our ability to achieve our goals during old age. Prudential rationality is usually thought of as having the goal of maximizing the amount of well-being in a life. If this is so, then prudential distribution throughout a single life should at least roughly match the utilitarian conclusion about transfers from the young to the old. The transfer should only be made if the loss involved for the young is less than the gain for the elderly. Consequently, according to Daniels's view, the elderly will only be treated unfairly if they have less than utilitarianism would assign to them.

This underestimates the claims of the elderly. If the elderly are very badly off and the members of the later generation are reasonably affluent, resources should be transferred from the young to the old. This judgment was shared by the creators of social security. One of their aims was to alleviate distress among the elderly, not just to distribute resources in the maximally efficient way. Utilitarianism might not recommend such transfers; it is hard to help the very old. Their age and the physical and psychological problems it creates make it difficult for them to make use of resources to improve the quality of their lives. Like the handicapped, they count as exceptions to the principle of diminishing marginal utility. For the same reason, the prudential chooser would not choose to place aside the quantity of resources for her old age that it would be right for us to provide to those who are old and living in hardship.

Consider the people described in Philip Larkin's grim poem "The Old Fools":

> Or do they fancy there's really been no change,
> And they've always behaved as if they were crippled or tight,
> Or sat through days of thin continuous dreaming
> Watching the light move?...
>
> . . . .

...And these are the first signs:
Not knowing how, not hearing who, the power
Of choosing gone.[8]

People in that condition will not be easy to help in a meaningful
way. There is a case for giving residents in nursing homes decent, or
more than decent, surroundings. But how much good will it do? A
nicely furnished television room does little for the mentally incompetent, and the people who could enjoy it may often be reluctant
to use it, because of the presence of the others. Yet to many of us,
the effort and the expense are worth making, despite the limited
benefits. We think that it is especially important to do what we can
for people who are old and suffering hardship.

This concern could not be explained by utilitarianism supplemented by diminishing marginal utility, and it requires a principle
focused on a temporal part of a life. The elderly are sometimes
among the worst off, and that is why we want to help them.
However, the resources given to them might produce more happiness if they were assigned to the young. So we must appeal to
a principle that would prefer benefits for them even when others
could be benefited more. Neither the prudential lifespan account
nor straightforward utilitarianism can draw this conclusion.

3.3 WHY PRUDENCE?

I have criticized the prudential lifespan account by arguing that
it generates conclusions that are intuitively unacceptable. There

8. Philip Larkin, *Collected Poems* (London: Marvell Press and Faber and Faber, 1988,
196–97).

is another question that should be raised about that theory. Why should we think that a prudential judgment made about a single life provides the key to understanding justice between the young and the old?

The writers who adopt this view think that there should be a theory of justice between age groups, with principles that are distinct from other kinds of justice. They are not satisfied by complete lives egalitarianism. They agree that justice between age groups is concerned with temporal parts of lives not lifetimes, even if their theory starts from a judgment about a complete life.

If there is a distinctive story about justice between age groups, why should we think that we discover it by an appeal to prudence? Daniels emphasizes the advantages of the prudential distribution: It will benefit everyone over time by making their complete lives better. This is important, but it does not explain why we should regard a departure from the prudential distribution as an injustice rather than a merely inefficient use of resources. He also points out that the prudential distribution that assigns more to some temporal stages of lives than to others will not produce inequalities between complete lives. This explains why the prudential distribution will not violate principles of justice for lifetimes, but it does not explain why we should appeal to prudence when we are thinking about justice between temporal parts of lives. The prudential lifespan account proper is concerned with the temporal parts of lives, not with lifetimes.

The prudential distribution over temporal parts of lives might give one person little and someone else a great deal and we might think that this is not fair.

Daniels believes that the distribution between age groups does not cross the boundaries between lives, which is why the appeal to prudence is unproblematic. But in one clear sense the distribution chosen by prudence does cross the boundaries between lives, dividing health care resources between the young and the old. Daniels suggests that prudence does not cross the boundaries between lives in a way that is morally objectionable. His reason for thinking that his theory passes this test again seems to be the compatibility of the appeal to prudence with equality among lifetimes. However, that reason only supports Daniels's conclusion about the innocuousness of the appeal to prudence if we suppose that the only morally important temporal units that we need to consider are lifetimes.

But his theory is concerned with temporal parts of lives. If it makes sense to apply equality to temporal stages of lives, then prudence might cross the boundaries between lives in an objectionable way even though it preserves equality between complete lifetimes.

The prudential lifespan account, in the end, makes claims about interpersonal justice, telling us to benefit one person rather than another when distributing resources across temporal parts of lives, even if this choice will not introduce inequality between complete lives. The decision to implement the prudential distribution has interpersonal implications: We refuse to benefit one person in order to benefit another. Daniels wants to have it both ways: treat the choice being made as not fully interpersonal when it is a matter of trying to justify the appeal to prudence but still regard the prudential choice as uncovering a special kind of interpersonal justice.

Since Daniels's view is distinct from complete lives egalitarianism, to defend it we must also answer the arguments in chapter 2 that showed that complete lives egalitarianism is sufficient. Obviously, the prudential lifespan account is immune to the argument from prudence. The theory cannot conflict with prudential thinking, but the prudential lifespan account is apparently vulnerable to the argument from compensation, the argument about responsibility, and the argument that lifetimes are the only suitable temporal scope for egalitarian principles because of the unity of a life. Before we adopt the prudential lifespan account, we need to find answers to these arguments.

I have brought intuitive objections and theoretical objections against the prudential lifespan account. The intuitive objections claim that the appeal to prudence will lead to conclusions that we will find repugnant. The theoretical objections question the status of the prudential lifespan account as a theory of justice that is intrinsically concerned with parts of lives rather than lifetimes. Although there are obvious reasons for distributing across age groups in the way that prudential thinking would recommend in the case of a single life, it is not clear why the conclusions the view reaches should be regarded as having the status of claims of justice. Because the prudential lifespan account in its own way makes the concern for complete lifetimes fundamental, it is not clear how it can resist the simpler view that justice is only concerned with lifetimes. If the theory tells us to distribute resources across temporal stages of lives in the way that would maximize the good of the complete life that contained those stages, it is natural to ask whether we are really giving independent moral importance to the temporal stages of lives themselves.

I am not claiming that the objections refute the prudential lifespan account or, more generally, the appeal to prudence as a way of arriving at a theory of justice between age groups. For one thing, the prudential lifespan account attempts to maximize the well-being that people will experience over their lives as wholes, and this consideration is undeniably a relevant and important reason in distributing between age groups (even if we do not agree that it is the only reason). However, I hope the objections give rise to considering an alternative approach to justice between the young and the old that might avoid the difficulties that arise for Daniels's theory.

Chapter 4

Equality

The prudential lifespan account proposes that we discover principles of justice for age groups—principles that apply to the people of different ages who constitute the age groups—by thinking about a single life. The principles are ultimately based in prudential concern for the overall quality of a complete human life.

I suggest instead that we will find these principles by comparing the temporal stages in different lives. The principles are not explained by prudence. They are a special application of a value that is more directly related to distributive fairness, one that would typically be used in making decisions that affect the lives of different people. The application is special because the value is applied to temporal parts of lives, not to complete lives.

Two aspects of this suggestion distinguish it from the basic assumptions that motivate the prudential lifespan account. The first is that we preserve the idea that the issue we are concerned with is an interpersonal rather than an intrapersonal one. We should continue to regard the temporal stages in question as belonging to different lives led by different people, rather than engaging in Daniels's shift of perspective and thinking of them as though they were sequential stages in the same lifetime. Second, we should think about the temporal stages themselves rather than switching to thinking about a complete lifetime and considering how its overall quality could be maximized. We should apply the moral values in question directly to temporal stages of lives themselves, in a way that is guided by how well or badly people are faring during those temporal parts of their lives rather than by how well or badly they fare over their lives as wholes.

We should move away from, or rather supplement, the complete lives view. There is a consideration of justice that is discovered by thinking about life stages rather than lifetimes. When we understand this consideration, we will see that it has the strongest claim to be the principle of justice distinctively concerned with age groups.

Because the view has these two features, it differs substantially from the prudential lifespan account. There is no reason to think that it will reach the same conclusions.

There are two ways of explaining the claims of fairness I described. Suppose we compare the current temporal stage in the life of someone who is old with the current temporal stage in the life of someone who is young, and the older person is much worse off. One explanation is that we are concerned by the current inequality between them. The inequality is between the current stages of their lives, not between their lifetimes. We may find this inequality objectionable for its own sake, even if their lifetimes turn out to be equal. So we might favor a transfer of resources from the younger person to the older one during the current temporal stages of their lives in order to reduce this inequality, even if the resources would do more good if they were left with the younger person.[1]

---

1. Of course it is also possible for the elderly to have too large a share when we compare their present status to that of other age groups. In Canada and the United States, we increasingly find rough equality between the old (excluding the "old old") and the young. Few would claim that this equality between the current stages of the lives of the young and the elderly is unfair in and of itself (although if I am right about the distributive conclusions that the prudential lifespan account would support, Daniels's theory

Moreover, I am also supposing that sometimes we might transfer resources to reduce the present inequality even if it means that the younger person will fare worse than the older person in terms of complete lives. If we agree, it shows that our concern is with equality between temporal stages in lives, not with inequality between lifetimes.

The second possibility is that we may think that helping the older person takes priority over helping the younger person. We may think that it is more urgent and more important to benefit the older person, because she is worse off, even if we could benefit the younger person more. We are more likely to think this when the older person is extremely badly off in an absolute sense, not just worse off than the younger person.

The priority view holds that a benefit experienced by someone who is badly off has special value, just because that person is badly off. Unlike the concern for equality, it does not focus on the relationship between the lives of different people. It considers the absolute condition of the person who is badly off and holds that, in virtue of that condition, it is especially important to help that person. This view sees more value in giving a benefit to the badly off person than in bestowing it on a person who is better off. If we accept this view we will often, but not always, reduce inequality, not because inequality as such counts as something bad, but because it is more important to increase the badly off person's level of well-being than to increase the better-off person's level of well-being, when we value well-being in the appropriate way.

would be committed to this claim). If we, nevertheless, believe that the elderly have too large a share, it will be because of a concern with equality in terms of complete lives between the members of the birth-cohort that now constitutes the age group of the elderly and the members of later generations.

This kind of priority might require a well-off younger person to surrender resources to an elderly person who is currently badly off, even if the complete life of the younger person will turn out to be worse overall than the complete life of the elderly person. If we awarded priority only on the basis of lifetimes and gave priority to helping the person with the worst complete life, the transfer would be rejected. If we support the transfer, we are assigning priority to the person whose life has the worst temporal stage and claiming that it is especially important to benefit that person when she is badly off. This would show that our concern is for a temporal stage in a life, not for a lifetime.

Both the view about equality and the view about priority allow us to respond directly to the condition that some peoples' lives are in when they are old. The response is not mediated by first comparing complete lifetimes and then deciding on that basis whether they deserve to be helped. According to these views, the misery that the people feel when they are old can itself provide us with a reason, and a reason of justice, to help them.

The examples that have already been discussed provide intuitive support for these views.[2] I think we can also discern these values behind some of the policies of the institutions that distribute

2. It might seem that there is a third value that could be used to account for the judgments I am trying to explain, the value of sufficiency, which could also be applied to temporal parts of lives, as well as to complete lifetimes. Sufficiency would require that we should ensure that a person should enjoy at least a specified minimum of well-being during every stage of her life. (Someone who held this view could agree that sufficiency must compete with other values and that sometimes it might not determine all things considered judgments.) Some might find such a view attractive, partly because the notions of sufficiency that have been formulated seem to make less strong demands than views based on equality or priority. (As in the case of equality and priority, those views often have not carefully distinguished between sufficiency applied to lifetimes and sufficiency applied to people at particular times). However, I will not discuss at length a view applying sufficiency to temporal parts of lives. This is partly because I find the usual sufficiency views intuitively implausible and, more importantly, because I think that sufficiency is best understood as a special case of the value of priority.

between the young and the old. The notion of what was called the "adequacy" of social security benefits played a key role in debates about American social security in the 1930s, 1940s, and 1950s. Social security was designed as a contributory pension plan in which the benefits that people received would match or be proportionate to their contributions to the system (this consideration was called equity). However, the system also was set the task of providing retired people with at least an adequate standard of living, even in the case of those who had made only minimal contributions. The view was that their lives during old age should meet at least a minimum standard of quality, and that goal was given priority by the institution.[3]

During the 1960s, social security regularly increased the benefits for retirees. This broached even further the proportionality between peoples' contributions and what they received. One justification for the increases was sharing the increasing prosperity of the era with those who had already retired. This might be interpreted as having the goal of reducing the current inequality between age groups. If so, it was a case of caring about inequality between life stages.[4]

---

3. "[I]ts [social security's] first objective in the manner of benefits should, therefore, be that those covered by it will, so far as possible, be assured of that minimum income which in most cases will prevent their becoming a charge on society." Reinhard A. Hohaus, "Equity, Adequacy, and Related Factors in Old Age Security," *Record of the American Institute of the Actuaries* 27, no. 55 1938 62. As the quote implies, Hohaus believed that adequacy was more important than equity. I do not mean to suggest that this conception of a bare minimum is the appropriate goal for social security. We might instead use a more flexible notion of priority that would award at least some priority to people who were living well above the level that Hohaus seems to be trying to pick out.

4. For an insightful—if highly critical—discussion of the ideas about fairness, equity, and adequacy that were actually used by the managers of American social security, see Martha Derthick's excellent study *Policy Making for Social Security* (Washington, DC: The Brookings Institution, 1979, chapters 10–13). My discussion of the historical illustrations suggests that over time an appeal to equality tended to replace an appeal to

In the case of both equality and priority, the fact that we would not choose to help the person who can be benefited the most shows that the value we are using is one concerned with distributive fairness, not just the maximizing consideration of producing the greatest amount of whatever is good. The fact that we would not choose to help the person who has the strongest claim in terms of complete lives shows that this value is concerned with temporal stages of lives, not lifetimes.

This is another difference between the prudential lifespan account and the views that I defend. The prudential lifespan account is set within the framework of a theory of justice concerned with lifetimes. As I explained in chapter 3, the principles of the frame theory outweigh the principles dealing with temporal parts of lives. As a consequence, although Daniels can give independent importance to achieving fairness between temporal parts of lives, he cannot allow that this could be more important than achieving fairness in terms of lifetimes. The views I defend allow that the moral concerns based on life stages might sometimes outweigh the concerns based on lifetimes. At least there seems to be no fundamental objection to formulating the views in this way, and we should make use of this possibility.

Both equality and priority are egalitarian values in the broad sense of the term.[5] So in saying that one or both of the two will be

priority. I think that this is a reasonable view, but I will not attempt to argue for it as an historical claim. One complication is that the generation (in the sense of birth-cohort) who retired in the 1960s would typically also have had worse complete lives than the members of younger age groups, so the case is not a pure example of caring about equality between life stages rather than lifetimes.

5. Some philosophical writers restrict the term *egalitarian* to the concern for equality. They contend that the priority view should not be counted as an egalitarian moral theory. Their reason is in part etymological, but more seriously, they want to emphasize the fundamental difference between equality that cares about relations between lives and priority that cares about the absolute condition of lives. I think we can use "egalitarian" to cover both views while still appreciating the depth of the difference between them.

included in an account of justice between age groups, I am endorsing egalitarianism. The points about social security might help to explain, if they do not justify, my choice.

Nevertheless, it remains tempting to think that moral concerns need only consider lifetimes. So defending my account requires explaining how the values of equality and priority can be applied to temporal parts of lives rather than to lifetimes.

In this chapter, I make a case for the application of equality to temporal parts of lives, and I try to answer the objections to it (as discussed in chapter 2).[6] However, there are serious problems for this application of equality. In chapter 5, I explain and defend the application of priority to temporal parts of lives. I argue that it is more convincing than the application of equality.

The case for thinking that inequality among parts of peoples' lives can be objectionable for its own sake begins with examples in which we are intuitively troubled by this kind of inequality even if it is compensated for over the course of lifetimes. The nursing home and condominium example can play that role, but it is more persuasive if the case involves even more extreme inequality. The example of changing places egalitarianism—a society practicing slavery in which slaves and masters change places every 20 years so there is always extreme inequality between parts of lives but

Some writers who are thought of as influential defenders of egalitarianism are actually advocating a version of the priority view.

6. I have discussed these applications in journal articles. For equality, see "Equality and Time," *Ethics* 99, 1989, 475–91. For the notion of egalitarian priority applied to temporal parts of lives (I call this the time-specific priority view), see "Justice between the Young and the Old," *Philosophy & Public Affairs* 30, 2002, 153–77. Larry Temkin discusses applying equality to temporal parts of lives in chapter 8 of his book *Inequality* (Oxford, UK: Oxford University Press, 1993, 233–44)). Daniels comments on this view in "The Prudential Life-Span Account of Justice across Generations," *Justice and Justification: Reflective Equilibrium in Theory and Practice* (Cambridge: Cambridge University Press, 1996, 264–69), and Kappel writes about the application of both values to temporal parts of lives in "Equality, Priority, and Time," *Utilitas* 9, 1997, 203–25.

no inequality between complete lives—is one such case. Another example is Larry Temkin's variation on the biblical story of Job. God makes two people, Job 1 and Job 2, suffer as much as the original Job did. Over their lifetimes they experience equal amounts of suffering, but God alternates their periods of suffering so that, when Job 1 experiences 25 years of idyllic happiness, Job 2 feels unremitting agony. Their lifetimes are equal, but they are radically unequal during their lives.

The examples are not intended to show that the equality between lifetimes is unimportant. They are meant to persuade us that we object to inequality between stages of lives—or at least to extreme inequality between stages of lives—even when it is accompanied by equality between lifetimes. The conclusion the examples support is that, although equality between lifetimes might be important, it would be better to also have rough equality between stages in lives.

One response to the examples is to admit that they have intuitive force but to argue they should not convince us that inequality between life stages is objectionable for its own sake. The examples are objectionable, but their wrongness can be explained in other ways.[7] Slavery involves the violation of fundamental rights. In Temkin's example, God is grossly mistreating both Jobs by exposing them to undeserved suffering. Deep inequality between parts of lives can have bad consequences apart from the inequality itself, and these consequences might be our real reasons for objecting.

To meet this worry, consider a less extreme example: a marriage in which the partners share throughout is better than a marriage in which one partner leads while the other follows at any

---

7. Temkin mentions this possible reply in footnote 8 on page 237 but does not attempt to answer it.

given time, even if his or her shares in power and authority turn out to be equal over the marriage as a temporal whole. In the second marriage, the division of authority at particular times does not amount to domination versus subservience, and the marriage does not involve anything that could plausibly be regarded as a rights violation.[8] Nevertheless, I think we would see the second marriage as inferior to the first. This example resists the alternative explanations previously suggested.

A different criticism holds that the conclusions I have drawn on the strength of the examples only seem persuasive because of certain attitudes that we have in regard to time. We might choose to help someone who is badly off now, even if in the past that person was much happier than other people. This is not because we object to inequality between the current stage of his life and the current stages of other lives, but because we think, reasonably or unreasonably, that the past no longer matters. The person's happiness is a fact about the past, so we do not take it into account in deciding how we should treat him now.

However, this proposal cannot account for all of our judgments. Some of the intuitively persuasive examples involve a difference between the past and the present or future, but we are also disturbed by deep inequality between different parts of lives if that inequality is in the future. I will argue that applying equality to stages in lives gives importance to facts about time, but it does not depend on a difference in our attitudes to the past as opposed to the present and the future.

There are three different ways of applying equality to temporal parts of lives.[9] The relevant comparisons are between the temporal

8. "Equality between age groups," *Philosophy and Public Affairs* 21, 1992, 275–95, see 289–90.
9. "Equality and Time."

parts of different lives, not between different temporal stages of the same life.

The first way assesses inequality by comparing a person's condition at a particular time to the conditions of other people at each temporal stage in their lives. Each temporal stage in a given life is compared to each temporal stage in each life. According to this view, any inequality that is discovered by these comparisons is objectionable. For example, inequality between the old age of one person and the simultaneous middle age of another person is objectionable, but the inequality would also be objectionable if the two temporal parts of the two lives were not lived simultaneously. I call this the total segments view.

Another way of assessing inequality compares a person's condition at a particular time to other peoples' conditions at that same time, so the comparison is always between the simultaneous states of different lives. If A is born (roughly) 25 years before B, A's middle age will be compared with B's youth, and if there is inequality, it is viewed as objectionable. However, if these two stages in different lives were not simultaneous, this view, which I call the simultaneous segments view, would not object to the inequality between them.

The third possibility is to compare a person's condition at a particular time to other peoples' conditions at stages in their lives that match, or correspond to, the stage that the first person is at. In chapter 2, I divided lives into the temporal stages of youth, middle age, and old age. For example, if the first person is young at the time in question, we might compare that person's condition to the conditions of others when they are or were young. I call this the corresponding segments view. It makes some comparisons between simultaneous stages in different lives, and it also makes some comparisons between nonsimultaneous stages of different lives.

Some think that that all three ways of applying equality to people at particular times have some prima facie plausibility.[10]

I believe that if there is morally significant inequality between parts of lives it is inequality between the simultaneous temporal stages of different lives. For example, inequality in the present between the old age of A and the middle age of B would matter, but not inequality between the matching but nonsimultaneous temporal stages of different lives like inequality between the old age of A during the 1990s and the old age of C during the 1970s. Inequality between stages that are not simultaneous and that do not correspond to one another would not matter.[11]

To begin with the strongest reason for defending my view, the most powerful examples of intuitively objectionable inequality between parts of lives involve simultaneous inequality. This is true of both my examples and Temkin's example of the two Jobs. In these cases, what matters most to us is that some are miserable while others flourish.

Some writers suggest that the corresponding segments view is also persuasive, perhaps even as persuasive as the simultaneous segments view. To test this claim, compare these two cases.

10. There is an independent discussion of different ways of thinking about equality in Marilyn Moon's "Measuring Intergenerational Equity" in *Justice Across Generations*, Lee Cohen, ed. (Public Policy Institute of the American Association of Retired Persons, 1993, 63–76). Moon calls inequality between complete lives "cohort differences," inequality between the corresponding segments of different lives "life stage differences," and inequality between simultaneous (but noncorresponding) segments of different lives "age inequality." She does not attempt to decide which of these inequalities matter.

11. I have earlier proposed a particular way of understanding the simultaneous segments view ("Equality and Time," 487–88). I suggested that it is in effect a disguised way of measuring the amount of inequality between complete lives or lifetimes. It claims that the inequality between two lifetimes equals the sum of the inequalities between the simultaneous parts of those lifetimes. I now think that this suggestion was mistaken. The simultaneous segments view is not a complicated way of caring about inequality

The numbers measure the welfare or well-being of the people A and B during the time periods T1, T2, T3, T4, and T5.

		T1	T2	T3	T4	T5
Case I:	A	5	5	1		
	B			5	5	1
Case II:	A	5	5	2		
	B			4	7	1

In case I, there seems to be a reason to transfer a unit from B to A during T3 to reduce simultaneous segments inequality, even though it would create inequality between their complete lives and also increase the corresponding segments inequality (this is not the claim that, all things considered, the transfer would be a good thing, since I also assume that we do care about inequality between lifetimes). However, in case II, there does not seem to be a reason to transfer a unit from A to B during T3 merely to reduce the corresponding segments inequality. This transfer would reduce inequality between A in T3 and B in T5, but it would also increase inequality between complete lives and increase simultaneous segments inequality. Some may think that these extra consequences of the transfer are masking the fact that there is a strong case for reducing corresponding inequality. However, I see no reason for thinking that this explains our judgment about the example.

between complete lives. It is fundamentally concerned with the temporal parts of lives as such and with inequality between parts of lives. One problem with my old view was that it implies that, in an example such as changing places egalitarianism, we can defensibly assert both that there is no inequality between peoples' lifetimes and that

Daniels and Temkin are among those who have at least some sympathy for the corresponding segments view.[12] Temkin discusses an example that is similar to the previous one:

		T1	T2	T3	T4	T5	T6
Case IV:	A	8	8	2	2		
	B	2	2	8	8		
Case VII:	A	8	8	2	2		
	B			2	2	8	8

The simultaneous segments view finds objectionable inequality in IV but not VII while the corresponding segments view finds objectionable inequality in both IV and VII.

Temkin does not see this example as helping us to decide in favor of the simultaneous segments view. However, this example also supports my conclusion. There is no objectionable inequality

there is a great deal of inequality between lifetimes. Given this change in my view, I now believe that if we accept the simultaneous segments view we must be willing to say that inequality between temporal parts of lives can matter in addition to, and independently of, inequality between lifetimes.

12. Daniels, "The Prudential Lifespan Account of Justice across Generations," 257–83; Temkin, *Inequality*, 240–42. In the case of Daniels, this sympathy is easy to understand. If we suppose that the frame theory of justice calls for equality between people's lifetimes, then Daniels's own view—the prudential lifespan account—would entail the corresponding segments view. The frame theory calls for equal shares for different people in terms of complete lives, and the prudential choice determines a proportion that should hold in each life between its different temporal stages. These two ideas together would require equality between the childhoods of different people, their middle years, and so on. However, the reverse entailment does not hold. The corresponding segments view does not require that the distribution over noncorresponding stages of lives should match the choice that prudence would make if the segments

in case VII, but perhaps there is in case IV. There might be a reason for a transfer from B to A during T4 in case IV, even though it would create inequality between their complete lives (again, this is not to say that, all things considered, the transfer would be a good thing). By contrast, there is no reason for a transfer from A to B during T4 in case VII in order to reduce corresponding segments inequality.

This second transfer would reduce the corresponding segments inequality between A in T2 and B in T4, but it would also increase the corresponding segments inequality between A in T4 and B in T6. Once again, someone might think that this is why we do not see the need for a transfer from A to B during T4 in case VII. To remove this possible explanation of our judgment, I do not see a reason for switching B's welfare levels during T4 and T6 (that is, making B's level in T4 8 and in T6 2) to reduce the corresponding segments inequalities between A in T2 and B in T4 and between A in T4 and B in T6.

In discussing these examples, I am assuming that if we apply equality to particular times we will sometimes conclude that a reduction in inequality between parts of lives can be more important than a reduction in inequality between lifetimes. So before endorsing the corresponding segments view it is important to ask whether we would reduce corresponding segments inequality at the cost of increasing lifetime inequality. This question has a strong effect on my own judgments. It is persuasive to claim that we should sometimes reduce simultaneous segments inequality even

belonged to the same life. There is no such positive connection between the prudential lifespan account and the simultaneous segments view, because Daniels's view does not require equality between the different temporal stages in a single life or between the simultaneous but noncorresponding stages in different lives.

if it creates or increases inequality between lifetimes. However, it is not reasonable to transfer resources from a middle-aged person to a young person merely to create equality between their respective youths, if this would also create inequality between their complete lives that otherwise would not have existed.[13]

The total segments view has the advantage of simplicity and generality. It applies equality to parts of lives across all times, in that it compares a temporal stage in one life to all the temporal stages in other lives, whether they are simultaneous or nonsimultaneous, corresponding or noncorresponding. One consequence of the generality is that the total segments view does not make facts about time intrinsically morally important. For example, the view does not give importance to the fact of simultaneity in the way that the simultaneous segments view does. It also does not agree with the corresponding segments view in giving importance to what might be regarded as a different kind of fact about timing, the temporal ordering of the different stages inside a life—different in that it involves the relation of temporal succession, rather than the notions of past, present, and future. Finally, the total segments view applies equality to stages of lives in the way that the value of priority should be applied to stages of lives. If we believe that the values of equality and priority are closely linked, this will also seem to count in favor of the total segments view. If that way of applying priority to temporal stages of lives is reasonable, how could it be clearly unreasonable to apply equality in the same way?

13. In her paper, Marilyn Moon suggests that avoiding corresponding segments inequality (or life stage differences, in her terminology) is a reasonable goal of a social security system, although perhaps not as important a goal as avoiding inequality between lifetimes. Unfortunately, she does not give examples of policies that were adopted partly to achieve the first goal. Views that try to promote equality of opportunity might want

However, the total segments view has little intuitive support. Like the corresponding segments view, it objects to inequality between corresponding but nonsimultaneous parts of different lives. This means that the points that I have made against the corresponding segments view will also apply to it. For example, we are not inclined to think that the inequality between A's youth and B's youth in case II would be objectionable unless it contributed to inequality between lifetimes. This view objects to inequality between stage of lives that are neither simultaneous nor corresponding, and this is perhaps the least intuitive objection.[14]

Finally, suppose that two people are born on the same day, die on the same day, and on every intervening day in their lives their levels of well-being are perfectly equal. This case seems to be a paradigm of equality, and both the corresponding segments view and the simultaneous segments view would find nothing objectionable in it. However, the total segments view would object (for example) to noncorresponding and nonsimultaneous inequality holding between the first person on September 13, 1971, and the second person on October 31, 1995. This objection seems to me implausible in the extreme.

My aim in considering these examples was to make a case that the simultaneous segments view was the only intuitive way

there to be equality, at least in certain respects, between the childhoods of different people, even if they belong to different generations. However, I think that these views would ultimately treat equality of this sort as a means to an end that was concerned with people's lifetimes.

14. It is worth mentioning that the total segments view would also object to inequality between the different temporal parts of the same life, unless we were to add a condition to the view restricting it to cases involving different people (chapter 5 says more about applying equality inside a life). This objection has even less intuitive support. The question does not arise for the simultaneous segments view or the corresponding segments view because they cannot be applied to one life.

of applying equality to temporal parts of lives. The rest of my discussion of applying equality to parts of lives will deal with that view.[15]

First, if we decide to apply equality to stages of lives, we should also apply it to lifetimes. We could not object only to inequality between the simultaneous temporal parts of lives. The simultaneous segments view does not see any difference existing between the following two cases:

		T1	T2	T3	T4
Case I:	A	2	2	2	2
	B	8	8	8	8
Case II:	A	2	8	2	8
	B	8	2	8	2

According to the view, the inequality in case I is no more objectionable than the inequality in case II, but surely an egalitarian should find case I to be more objectionable.

The problem is that the simultaneous segments view does not treat peoples' complete lives as being morally significant units. It is only concerned with minimizing the inequality between simultaneous parts of different lives. As the example shows, the

15. If we only accept the simultaneous segments view, it will follow that if two lives do not overlap temporally, so that none of their temporal parts are simultaneous, then our only concern will be with inequality between lifetimes, not with inequality between stages of the two lives. This consequence does not seem to me to be implausible.

distribution that minimizes the inequality between two people over a series of particular times may leave the same person worse off at each particular time, and this would clearly be wrong.[16]

To better understand the simultaneous segments view, it will help to consider the attitude it takes to the reductions that motivate the prudential lifespan account and similar accounts of justice between age groups. The prudential lifespan account claims that a synchronic, interpersonal question of distribution reduces to a diachronic, intrapersonal question of distribution. It also claims that a question about distribution between stages in lives reduces to a question about lifetimes. In virtue of these two reductions, the account also claims that the answer to the synchronic, interpersonal question about justice or fairness is arrived at through prudential thinking.

From the point of view of the simultaneous segments view, the reductions will seem to be mistakes. The simultaneous segments view holds that there are claims of fairness relevant to distribution between the simultaneous temporal parts of different lives. The view does not hold that there are claims of fairness governing distribution between the distinct, nonsimultaneous temporal parts of one and the same life. Consequently, the simultaneous segments view will claim that the replacement of the synchronic, interpersonal question by the diachronic, intrapersonal question is a mistake because to do so will ignore the claims that apply to distribution between the simultaneous temporal parts of different lives. We will not recognize these claims if we imagine the

---

16. A similar problem would arise for the suggestion that we only care about inequality between corresponding segments of lives. The total segments view does not face the same problem, since the distribution that minimizes the inequality between all of the temporal parts of two lives would also be the distribution that minimizes the inequality between the two lifetimes. However, if we extended the total segments view so that

temporal parts as the diachronically ordered segments of one and the same life. So Daniels's change of perspective conceals the very moral claims that we are searching for.

Because of the failure of this initial reduction, according to the simultaneous segments view, there is no reason to think that the answer to the question about the fair distribution between the simultaneous temporal stages in different lives will be ultimately found by thinking about complete lifetimes. Similarly, there is no reason to believe that the right answer to the question about distributive fairness will match the distribution that prudence would choose when it imagines the temporal parts as belonging to the same life and thinks about how to maximize its overall quality.

Hopefully it is clear why the simultaneous segments view— and the other views that apply equality to temporal parts of lives— escape the intuitive objections that were brought against the prudential lifespan account in chapter 3. Those views recognize a claim to equality between the temporal parts of different lives. They can hold that there is a claim to equality between the old age of the people in the nursing home and the middle age of the people in the condominiums, even if prudence would only have saved a limited amount of resources for extreme old age. So the views can support a transfer of resources from the young to the old, despite the fact that the resources would have produced larger gains of well-being if they had been left with the younger people. However, before deciding that this transfer was right, we would also have to take into account the size of the gains the younger people would experience (if the gains were large enough they might outweigh the claim to equality), and the consideration of equality applied

---

it also applied to the different temporal parts of the same life, then this view would also not see an important difference between case I and case II in the text.

to lifetimes (if the transfer would give the younger people worse complete lifetimes than the people who are now old, the loss in terms of lifetime equality might outweigh the gain in terms of equality between life stages).

There are three central objections to the simultaneous segments view described in chapter 2—the argument about compensation, the argument about prudence, and the argument about responsibility (these objections would also arise for the total segments view and the corresponding segments view).

The simultaneous segments view objects to inequality between temporal parts of lives, even if this inequality does not result in inequality between lifetimes because the inequality is reversed at earlier or later times. But if the inequality is reversed at other times, then the person who is worse off at one particular time seems to be compensated for this relative disadvantage at some other time. Compensation means that the person is no worse off because of the pattern of inequality than he would have been without it. And if he is compensated, why should his initial disadvantage be a concern of justice?

Moreover, it is possible that every person might be better off over their lifetime as a whole because of simultaneous inequality between parts of their lives. If the inequality is compensated for and actually benefits everyone concerned in the long run, why should we complain?

My answer to the objection appeals to a particular view of the kind of value that equality is. The concern for equality for its own sake is a relative or comparative value. Someone who feels the concern objects to the differences between different lives, not to the damage that the inequality inflicts on those who are worse off under the inequality. This kind of egalitarian might object to lifetime inequalities that benefit the people who are the worst off, inequalities that Rawls's difference principle would permit. In the same way, it is possible to object to inequalities between temporal parts of lives even if they benefit everyone concerned. The harm experienced at one time may be compensated for by a benefit at some other time, in the sense that the person in question is not made worse off by receiving the harm and the benefit than he would have been if he had received neither. But this does not guarantee that there is compensation in another sense. It does not mean that the simultaneous inequality that the harm was part of is compensated for, or morally erased by, the opposite simultaneous inequality that the benefit is part of.[17] We might think that both inequalities still count as being wrong despite the fact that the harms are compensated for. We can take this view if we distinguish between the wrongfulness of inequality—which is created by the difference in quality between two peoples' lives—and the harm for one person that the inequality involves. Some egalitarians understand the wrongfulness of inequality between lifetimes in the first way, and we can take the same view about the wrongfulness of inequality between temporal parts of lives.[18]

So the argument from compensation can be answered if we are willing to care about equality in a certain way, that is if we are willing to care about relative differences between people (rather than harm). Some egalitarians do value equality in that way, as their

17. The argument about compensation assumes that, if the benefit compensates for the harm in the first sense, then it must also compensate in the second sense. It is fair to say that the argument begs the question against applying equality to temporal parts of lives.
18. This way of replying to the objection can be found in "Equality and Time," 487–88. However, it is important to remember that valuing equality for its own sake as a relation between lives does not commit us to objecting to simultaneous inequality between temporal parts of lives. Thinking about equality, we might simply decide that the later simultaneous inequality morally erases the former simultaneous inequality, independently of the argument about compensation. So an egalitarian might object

judgments about complete lifetimes make clear. But nonegalitarians strongly oppose that way of valuing equality, and even some egalitarians are reluctant to make these claims about the value of equality. Answering the objection in this way brings this strong commitment with it. It may make us hope to find another way of explaining our intuitive judgments about temporal parts of lives that would not involve the commitment.

Interpreted in this way, the simultaneous segments view takes a distinctive view of the case of a person making choices about his life. Sometimes a person can make his life better overall by creating great inequality between the temporal stages in his life. When only one person is involved, the view does not object to this choice. However, if a number of people make the same choice, the simultaneous segments view will object if the choice creates inequality between the simultaneous segments of different lives. So even if simultaneous segments inequality would make everyone better off in the long run, there could still be an objection to it.

My defence of the simultaneous segments view from the objection about compensation might make it seem extremely vulnerable to the objection based on prudence. The objection is most forceful if we think about an institution such as social security. The operation of the social security system over time will tend to create a certain distribution across the consecutive temporal stages of a single life and to create the same distribution across the simultaneous temporal stages of different lives. But prudence and the simultaneous segments view differ in terms of what this distribution should be. If social security aims at the distribution favored by prudence, it will violate the constraints of fairness imposed by

to inequality between complete lives that benefits the worse-off person but still not object to inequality between parts of lives for its own sake.

the simultaneous segments view. If, instead, it follows the simultaneous segments view, it will treat people in a way that prudence would object to, and the treatment might make everyone worse off in the long run.

Given that a deep conflict between prudence and the simultaneous segments view exists, there are different ways of dealing with it. One view would insist that considerations of justice, such as those expressed by the simultaneous segments view, should outweigh considerations about what would make people better off. We should respect the simultaneous segments view for the sake of fairness even if it makes everyone worse off.

This means that the simultaneous segments view would eliminate inequality between parts of lives by leveling down, even when the result was that everyone was worse off over their lives as wholes. Since the view claims that inequality between temporal parts of lives is undesirable for its own sake, it might recommend eliminating this inequality even if no one would be made better off in a particular segment of their life. Many would refuse to accept these judgments, and they might feel that there is no reason to level down when doing so would not even improve a particular stage in someone's life. So responding to the conflict in this way would make the view hard for many people to endorse.

It is more persuasive to think that the reasons provided by the simultaneous segments view have to be weighed against the benefits that people might receive if resources are unequally distributed. Fairness between age groups would not always dominate the reasons concerned with making peoples' lives better in the long run. If a moderate amount of simultaneous segments inequality would benefit most people, the inequality might be justified on balance.

However, even this more moderate view would still be rejected by many. In principle, the view might lead to leveling down in at least some cases. Critics would say that it is never right to reduce inequality between temporal parts of lives when doing so would make some worse off and benefit no one. We could weaken the view even further by adding a condition ruling out leveling down, but this seems to be admitting that the conflict between prudence and the simultaneous segments view should always be resolved in favor of prudence, and that would make the simultaneous segments view of questionable importance.

Another way of responding claims that inequality is not objectionable if it is voluntarily agreed to by the people who are worse off under the inequality. Many egalitarians make this claim about inequality between lifetimes, and we could apply this idea to inequality between the simultaneous temporal parts of lives. When there is a conflict between prudence and the simultaneous segments view, perhaps everyone would agree to accept beneficial inequalities between the temporal parts of lives. Then the inequalities would not be objectionable.

But this approach runs the risk of making the simultaneous segments view otiose. We would end up by accepting Daniels's conclusions, though for a more complicated reason. If people choose the inequalities recommended by prudence, this would be the result.

I think that the conflict with prudence is not a sufficient reason for abandoning the simultaneous segments view. But the conflict might call for an alternative view that can explain the persuasive intuitive judgments that the simultaneous segments view supports, without creating a direct clash between prudential judgments about one life and ethical judgments about fairness between the young and the old. Even egalitarians who are willing to defend leveling down in the case of inequality between lifetimes might prefer to find a view about temporal stages in lives that would as a matter of principle never endorse leveling down (as opposed to a view that, when combined with other principles, might never recommend leveling down, all things considered). In chapter 5, I explain a view that satisfies these conditions.

I have appealed to people's choices to defend the simultaneous segments view against the objection based on prudence. However, choice introduces another problem for the simultaneous segments view, the objection from choice and responsibility. This difficulty is independent of the conflict between simultaneous segments egalitarianism and prudence.

Many (but not all) egalitarians want to formulate their theory in a way that leaves room for the moral importance of choice and responsibility. This usually takes the form of adding the condition that inequalities that people have voluntarily chosen, or inequalities that the worse-off people are responsible for, are not objectionable (there are many different views about how the condition should be expressed, but it is not necessary to settle that question).

Sometimes the relevant choice or responsible action occurs immediately before the inequality. In other cases, the choice or responsible action might occur well before the inequality. This situation might be thought to pose a problem for simultaneous segments egalitarianism. The simultaneous segments view seems to regard a single life as made up of different life stages that have moral importance in their own right. Suppose that in one temporal stage of his life a person makes a choice that renders him worse off than others during a later stage of his life. Since the simultaneous segments view gives independent moral importance to stages of lives in assessing inequality, its condition about choice and responsibility might also deal with life stages. The condition would imply that the inequality between simultaneous life stages is not objectionable if the person who is worse off under the inequality made a choice during that stage of his life that brought on the inequality.

The problem is that, if the choice came in an earlier stage of his life, then it seems that the inequality will count as objectionable, at least if he now regrets his earlier choice. Most people, and many egalitarians, would feel that this view must be rejected because it does not make people sufficiently responsible for the course of their own lives. The difficulty has a special relevance to the institutions and policies I am writing about. Suppose that in the example of the nursing home and the condominiums the people who are now elderly are entirely responsible for the conditions they find themselves in. They made no attempt to prepare for or to save for their old age, even though they had ample resources and opportunity to do so. It seems wrong to say that their responsibility for their condition does not in any way affect the duty of other people to help them now. Yet the simultaneous segments view is committed to that conclusion, if it assesses responsibility in terms of life stages.

However, simultaneous segment egalitarianism is not forced to draw these conclusions. It gives independent moral importance to temporal parts of lives in one specific way. The view supposes that inequality between the simultaneous temporal parts of different lives has independent moral importance. This does not mean that temporal parts of lives will turn out to have other kinds of moral importance. In particular, it does not commit us to thinking that responsibility needs to be made relative to temporal stages in lives. The simultaneous segments view is supported by plausible judgments about inequality, but the parallel judgments about responsibility are not persuasive. It does not seem reasonable to say that if the current stage of my life is profoundly affected by a choice that I made in some earlier stage, then I have no responsibility for accepting the consequences of my past choice.

A proponent of the simultaneous segments view can think about responsibility in the same way that lifetime egalitarians do. If the residents of the nursing home brought about their own misfortune by foolish decisions made earlier in life, this can eliminate or reduce the obligation to help them now. This concession does not undermine the basic idea of the simultaneous segments view. Someone who holds it will believe that when concerns about responsibility do not arise then inequality between stages of lives can be objectionable just as inequalities between lifetimes can be.[19]

I could not give this answer to the objection if applying equality to temporal stages in lives depended on denying that it is one and the same person who is first young and then old. Challenging the ordinary understanding of personal identity can support the application of equality to life stages, but it also supports rejecting the notion that responsibility extends across the boundaries

---

19. Some of these claims may seem to clash with my criticisms in chapter 3 of using a prudential choice made early in life as the test of what justice requires for the elderly. However, the two discussions are about very different issues. If a person actually made Dworkin's choice about insurance and ended up in serious difficulties in old age, then the view about responsibility that I have explained might say that he is responsible for his problems and that he does not deserve help. Chapter 3 criticized the use of a hypothetical prudential choice as a test of how much a person is entitled to receive in old age, apart from issues of responsibility. A hypothetical choice employed in a philosophical theory does not establish actual responsibility for actual results that happened to match the content of the hypothetical choice, and Dworkin does not use it for that purpose. There is no inconsistency in rejecting the use of a hypothetical choice as a theoretical idea in an account of justice for age groups while thinking that a person who made real a choice might be responsible for the results.

between different life stages. However, in chapter 6, I argue that the simultaneous segments view does not depend on challenging the ordinary notion of personal identity.

The view faces other objections apart from the objections based on compensation, prudence, and responsibility.

Daniels points out that we do not intuitively object to every kind of simultaneous inequality between temporal parts of different lives. For example, we do not object to inequality in educational opportunity between the young and the very old. Also if two people are very well off during every temporal part of their lives, we probably would not worry about inequality between simultaneous parts of their lives. For example, suppose that they are at different stages in their successful careers with a company that promotes on the basis of seniority, and at a given time one person is extremely well off while the other is only very well off. Few would regard this as an injustice.

These objections could be met by restricting the simultaneous segments view so that it only objected to certain kinds of inequality. We might decide that only inequalities in certain kinds of goods or resources matter. I myself think that ultimately we should be concerned with inequality in well-being itself, not with inequalities in such resources as access to education (but many egalitarians would disagree). We might also decide that we should only object to inequalities in which the worse-off person is very badly off in absolute terms. Of course it would be challenging to defend these restrictions in detail. However, these problems are not unique to views concerned with inequality between temporal parts of lives. Arguably a concern with inequality between lifetimes would also have to be restricted in similar ways to be intuitively plausible.

Klemens Kappel asks whether we would eliminate simultaneous segments inequality if doing so would make everyone worse off. In his example, two people must suffer and suffer equally throughout one temporal stage of their lives. If the two stages of suffering occur at different times, the two people will suffer less; if the two stages are simultaneous, they will each suffer more. Would we schedule their periods of suffering to avoid simultaneous segments inequality at the price of greater suffering?

As Kappel recognizes, this example applies to the simultaneous segments view a more general objection that could be directed against any concern for equality for its own sake, the objection that Derek Parfit has named the leveling down objection. It applies to the simultaneous segments view. I have already argued that the view needs to distinguish between the value of eliminating inequality and the value of benefiting people in order to answer the argument about compensation. Many people find the leveling down objection convincing. Still, some egalitarians—thinking about inequality between lifetimes—deny that it shows that we should not value equality for its own sake. If the objection does not establish that, then it also does not refute the simultaneous segments view.[20]

However, Kappel's objection also has a different kind of force, apart from the issue of leveling down. Thinking about his example might make it seem arbitrary to restrict the concern for equality in the way the simultaneous segments view does. The view claims that inequality between the temporal parts of different lives is

---

20. For the sake of simplicity, I have not introduced the more subtle question of whether leveling down could create an outcome that was better in at least one respect, if not an outcome that was better overall. This question plays an important role in the general debate about leveling down. I am also not suggesting that if we are willing to accept leveling down in the case of complete lives, we are committed to adopting the simultaneous segments view and defending it against objections in the way I have described. Someone might think that inequality between lifetimes is wrong for its own sake

morally important, but only when those parts are simultaneous. This claim gives intrinsic moral importance to a fact about time. Why should we suppose that simultaneity has that kind of moral significance? By contrast, inequality between the complete lives of A and B seems to be important both when the two lives are simultaneous and when they are not (although some egalitarians would deny that the inequality matters if the two lives are widely separated in time). Why should inequality between the old ages of A and B only matter when they are simultaneous? Even if our intuitive judgments (or at least some of them) seem to support the simultaneous segments view, we may feel that we do not understand why the concern for equality between temporal stages of lives should take this form. Why should simultaneity be necessary for this kind of inequality to matter?

The problem becomes more serious when we ask whether it is reasonable to literally require equality at particular times. Suppose that A and B must both suffer terribly but only for a moment. Is there a serious reason to schedule the suffering to occur at precisely the same moment, to avoid simultaneous inequality? Most people (including me) would say no. The example seems to show that an inequality between two people that only lasts for a moment is not objectionable at all. But if this inequality is morally unimportant, why should we think that there is something wrong when the inequality lasts longer but does not result in inequality between lifetimes?

It is tempting to answer that the brief duration of the inequality is enough to explain why it does not matter at all or to say that our intuitive judgment about the example might, after all, be

---

and so be willing to accept leveling down, without thinking that inequality between temporal parts of lives is in any way objectionable.

compatible with the momentary inequality mattering at least a little bit. But I do not think that we should be satisfied with these replies.[21] Judging by the examples that egalitarian writers resort to, our intuitive egalitarian judgments about pain and suffering seem to be as strong as any egalitarian judgments that we make. Suffering is a morally serious thing even if it only lasts for a moment (in chapter 5, we see how the priority view can reflect its importance). Suppose that two complete lifetimes are the same except that the first life contains a brief moment of agonizing pain while the second life does not—there is no other inequality between them. This inequality is morally important and should be taken into account by a principle of equality concerned with lifetimes. If the simultaneous segments view is correct, the two momentary inequalities constituted by the nonsimultaneous pains would also matter despite their brevity. Nevertheless, we do not find them objectionable.

The same problem emerges from comments by Nagel about the roots of egalitarianism.[22] Nagel is responding to Parfit's view about the relationship between egalitarianism and theories of personal identity (an issue considered in chapter 6). Nagel claims that egalitarianism does not depend on views about the nature of personal identity through time. The egalitarian impulse can arise as long as we can distinguish between different people at a time, and we can understand the difference between two experiences being had by the same person and their being had by two different people. Nagel concludes that a view of personal identity will determine the temporal size of the units over which the egalitarian principle

---

21. I offered lame answers of this sort in "Equality and Time," 483–84.
22. "Equality" 124n 16.

operates, but this is the only significant connection between theories of personal identity and egalitarianism.

In his reply, Parfit points out that some views about personal identity might affect the importance that we give to the egalitarian principle, not just its temporal scope.[23] My first response to Nagel would be that he is begging the question against views that apply egalitarian values to temporal parts of lives by supposing that personal identity determines the temporal scope of egalitarian principles. Why might not some egalitarian concerns reasonably use temporal units of narrower scope than the complete lives of self-identical subjects of experience?

Still, Nagel is right about something important. His simple example is a legitimate instance of egalitarian concern, so it should exhibit the basic features of that concern. Suppose the two experiences are pains, and we strongly prefer that each person should experience one pain rather than that one person should feel both pains while the other feels no pain at all. We can also ask whether it is better for the two people to feel their pains simultaneously. If we care about equality in the way that the simultaneous segments view proposes, we should think that it is better for the pains to be simultaneous. But we have no serious inclination to make that judgment. Since Nagel's example is a fair test, this must be respected as evidence against the simultaneous segments view.

There is a second objection to the simultaneous segments view. The view does not give egalitarian principles the temporal scope of complete lifetimes. It applies the principles to temporal parts

23. *Reasons and Persons*, 342–43. In an example cruder than the cases that Parfit is considering, imagine that the two subjects of experience are organisms that are merely sentient and lack the capacity for higher cognitive functioning including memory. A view about the identity of these organisms through time (assuming that we ascribe personal identities to them at all) will be relevant to the plausibility of egalitarian concerns. In this case, we might not think that there is any morally important difference between

of lives—for example, to the temporal stage of old age. However, old age can include a significantly extended temporal stretch of a life, perhaps 30 years. Two people might be roughly equal in terms of the overall quality of their lives over that temporal period. But there might be deep simultaneous inequalities between them during shorter stretches of time within the 30 years, inequalities that balance out so that their lives are equal when assessed over the 30-year period. The simultaneous segments view objects to inequality between temporal parts of lives even though it is balanced out over a lifetime, so it seems it should find these shorter periods of inequality objectionable for their own sake, despite the fact that they are compensated for. So what temporal unit should the view use as the replacement for a complete life? Apparently any reasonably extended temporal unit will be vulnerable to the problem that it might contain simultaneous inequalities that it cannot count as being objectionable.

We might decide to ignore this worry and simply choose a temporal unit of a given length, for example, 30 years, on the understanding that we will refuse to count simultaneous inequalities within that unit. However, the choice of that particular unit will seem arbitrary. If we had chosen a 25-year unit instead, we might have gotten different results as to how much objectionable inequality there was. Even if we are satisfied with the 30-year unit, it can be applied to a life in different ways. In assessing two lives, we could use it to group together the years between 1970 and 2000, or the years between 1980 and 2010.[24] Again we might get different answers as to how much inequality

one of the creatures experiencing two intense pains at different times and each of them experiencing one intense pain.

24. I am supposing that we would add A's level of welfare at the times inside the unit, then add B's, and check for inequality between the totals. If we use a short temporal unit, we

there is depending on which grouping we use, given that we are not counting simultaneous inequality within the 30 years. I have talked about applying equality to old age, which we can again suppose is a period of roughly 30 years, but is this a better way of assessing inequality than dividing the life into a 30-year period that includes part of middle age as well as old age? These two divisions would partially overlap, but here, too, we might get different answers to the question of how much objectionable inequality there is. There seems to be no limit to the number of ways in which we could divide lifetimes to measure simultaneous inequality. Unless there is some way of establishing that a particular unit is the most appropriate one to use, it will be indeterminate how much simultaneous segments inequality there is.

One response to these problems would be to argue that ultimately the view is concerned with equality at a given time. The appropriate temporal scope for an egalitarian view is, at least in principle, a moment. We can characterize inequality using larger temporal units, but what we say about those units can be analyzed in terms of inequality holding between different people at particular moments. So simultaneous inequality between two people during their old age would be a matter of the sum of the inequalities holding between them at all the moments contained in the temporal stage of old age.

This response has the merit of choosing a temporal unit that at least does not seem arbitrary, but many will find it implausible. Some might think it is difficult to give any sense to the notion of the amount of well-being that a person experiences at a particular

might register more objectionable inequality than if we were to assess the same case using a longer unit.

moment. Apart from this concern, the response leads directly to an objection already discussed, that we do not think that there is anything wrong with merely momentary inequality between people.

The force of these objections is that although we might find the simultaneous segments view persuasive, the case for it is at best double edged. Despite the examples that support it, most of us are also inclined to feel real doubt about whether simultaneity can have the importance that the view gives to it, when we think reflectively about this issue.[25,26]

There is a final reservation to note about the simultaneous segments view. In defending it against criticisms, I have essentially argued that the objections do not show that caring about equality in this way is ruled out by the fundamental nature of egalitarian concern. But this does not provide a positive reason for caring about this kind of inequality. My case for the simultaneous segments view rests on an appeal to our intuitive judgments about particular examples, such as the case of the nursing home and the condominium complex.

The simultaneous segments view treats a temporal stage of a life as a locus for distribution, as a morally significant unit that

25. Suppose that we believe that A and B, two romantic poets, were exact contemporaries and that their lives exhibited extreme simultaneous inequality. When A triumphed, B was living in misery and vice versa, but their successes and failures balanced out over time with the result that their lifetimes were roughly equal. Then we learn that our history text was only partially accurate. The two poets lives' went as we had supposed, but A was born 25 years before B so that their periods of happiness and misery precisely coincided. There was actually no simultaneous inequality between them at all. Would we be relieved when we acquired this information?

26. It is important to understand that there is another way in which the simultaneous segments view does not make simultaneity important. It does not say that we should only be concerned, or should have more concern, with inequalities between parts of people's lives that hold now, in the present. If we have a choice between ending a small inequality in the present or preventing a more extreme inequality in the future, it tells us to prevent the future inequality. The view holds that agents should care in the same

possesses a claim to a fair distributive share.[27] I have not given any general argument that a temporal stage in a life should be regarded as such a locus of distribution. Someone may feel confident that the complete life of a self-identical human being is such a locus of distribution but not think the same is true of a temporal stage in a life (this concern is related to the argument from the moral unity of a life in chapter 2). It might be thought that I must give reasons for treating a stage in a life in that way—perhaps by arguing for a particular view of the nature of personal identity or by appealing to the special closeness of the psychological connections inside a temporal stage. These attempts to strengthen the case for regarding temporal stages as morally significant units will be considered in chapter 6.

The structure of my argument has been to first contend that the simultaneous segments view is the only persuasive way of applying equality to temporal parts of lives and then to suggest that, in the end, we should have serious reservations about this view. The argument does not refute the simultaneous segments view, but it might motivate us to look for an account of justice between age groups with fewer problems. I propose such a view in chapter 5.

way about past, present, and future simultaneous inequality, and in that sense it is time neutral. But the distinctive feature of the view is its claim that a difference in the quality of parts of different lives is objectionable if the parts are simultaneous but not if the parts are not simultaneous. That makes simultaneity—a fact or truth about timing—important in a different way. Nagel's simple case tends to show that we do not think that simultaneity matters in this second way.

27. If this is a fair statement of what the simultaneous segments view is doing, it allows us to restate the objection about arbitrariness. If a temporal stage in a life has this status, why should its claims only have force when we are comparing it to the simultaneous stages in other lives?

Chapter 5

Priority

5.1 UNDERSTANDING PRIORITY

I am not convinced that the objections raised in the previous chapter show conclusively that it is unreasonable to care about simultaneous segments inequality. Nevertheless, they are at least persuasive and might motivate us to build the account of justice between age groups around priority applied to temporal parts of lives.

I formerly believed that there was little point in debating whether the concern that we seem to have with temporal parts of lives was explained by equality or priority. I assumed that, if there was a way of deciding between the two explanations, it would be based on some general reason for thinking that one value was more reasonable than the other, a reason that would apply to moral concerns about lifetimes as well as to concerns about individual stages of lives. However I have changed my mind because of the problems in applying equality to parts of lives. Most of the reasons for preferring priority to equality concern only the application to stages of lives, and they do not show that it is more reasonable to apply priority rather than equality when we are thinking about lifetimes. Also, they are not related to the familiar reasons that some writers have for thinking that the concern for priority is more defensible than the concern for equality, for example, the consideration of avoiding the leveling down objection.

In this chapter I will explain egalitarian priority and how it can be applied to temporal parts of lives. I will argue that a view based on priority escapes the objections against applying equality to temporal parts of lives. The priority view was developed by Temkin and Parfit. Unlike equality, egalitarian priority is not a relative or comparative value. It is concerned with improving lives of low quality, not with changing the relationship between these lives and other lives. Its basic claim is that the value of a benefit depends, in part, on the quality of the life of the person who receives it. The worse the quality of the life, the more important or valuable the gain is. Consequently, a smaller gain for someone badly off can be more important than a larger gain for someone better off. The special value of the gain for the badly off person, or the degree of priority that is given to it, depends on the absolute condition of the badly off person, not on her relative position with respect to the better-off person. There is no reason to think the priority will be a matter of absolute priority. Even when egalitarian priority is taken into account, a small gain for someone badly off might count as being less important than a much larger gain for someone better off.

As a simple illustration of the priority view, suppose that we have constructed a scale of the well-being of a particular person. Well-being is measured by the numbers 0, 1, 2, 3, and so on. An increase in well-being from 0 to 1 is a gain of a certain amount of well-being, and an increase from 1 to 2 is an increase of the same amount of well-being. The priority view might say that the increase from 0 to 1 has the value of 1. So the priority view also involves a second scale of value. Crucially, the priority view might claim that an increase of well-being from 1 to 2 has less value than the increase from 0 to 1. For example, it might say that the increase in well-being from 1 to 2 only contributes .95 on the scale of value, not 1. It might also claim that the value of successive increases of well-being will continue to diminish (of course the assignment of specific numbers on both scales is artificially precise). The value of a gain of well-being is inversely proportional to the amount of well-being that the person's life already contains. This is just one version of a priority view, and we could construct other versions by utilizing different relationships between the two scales. The fact that I have characterized the priority view by discussing a single life indicates that priority is not a relative or comparative concern.

Priority can be applied to complete lifetimes or to temporal stages of lives. The difference between the applications lies in the level of well-being that is relevant—the first application uses a measure of a person's well-being over their lifetime as a whole, while the second application uses the level of well-being during a particular stage of the life or at some particular time in the life.

In the first application, the person with the worst overall life has a strong claim to special consideration. A smaller benefit for him might outweigh a larger benefit for another person whose life regarded as a whole is better. In the case of priority based on a lifetime, the special claim still has force even if the person would receive the benefit at a particular time when he was relatively well off. In the case of priority based on a temporal stage of a life, it is a person whose current level of welfare is low who has a special claim to help. But the claim only has force if the benefits would be received when he was badly off, not if they are experienced at other times when he was faring well. The special claim to help when he is badly off still exists even if the person's life assessed as a whole is not worse than the lives of others.

To the extent that the distinction between these two applications has been clearly drawn, egalitarian writers seem to be more concerned with priority applied to lifetimes rather than priority applied to temporal parts of lives. However, when those writers give examples to support their view, they often appeal to cases where we are asked to give priority to someone who is currently badly off. For example, we might be asked to agree that it is more important to help someone who is experiencing agonizing suffering rather than helping a second person who is suffering less, even if we could eliminate a larger amount of pain if we helped the second person. The writers do not focus on a person with a life that is of poor quality overall and then claim that we should give priority to helping this person even if he will be benefited at a time when he is well off. This provides some evidence that we are inclined to apply the notion of priority to temporal parts of lives.

It is important to avoid one misunderstanding of this kind of priority view. The view does not tell us that we should be especially concerned with helping whoever is worst off at the present time. If the view took that form, it would give weight to the fact of simultaneity, although in a different way than the simultaneous segments view does. But the view is not time relative. Its judgments are explained by facts about the person who would be benefited. Benefits for people who are especially badly off when the benefit is received have a special value that is, in a sense, timeless. There is a reason for acting to benefit the person who counts as being the worst off, even if that person would be benefited at some time in the future. So if I must choose between helping the person who is worst off now or waiting and helping someone else a year from now who will then be even worse off, I should make the second choice. The fact that a person is suffering now does not give me an extra reason to help her. The strength of her claim depends on her current level of welfare and how much good the help would do her. It competes on that basis against the claim of a person I could help in the future.

Some may doubt whether there are realistic examples in which we are strongly inclined to apply priority to people at particular times rather than to lifetimes. The familiar moral concern with poverty is one such example. Many people believe that it is especially important and urgent to help those living in poverty. They think that it is more important to benefit the poor in a small way (but not a trivial way) than to create larger benefits for much better-off people. For example, they support social programs that are designed to help the poor even if those programs bring about little significant improvement in the lives of those they want to help. I think their concern is best understood as an example of egalitarian priority. The basic thought is that benefits for the poor have a special value, and they have this value because the lives of the poor are of low quality in an absolute sense.

The same example illustrates how priority focused on particular periods can compete with priority concerned with complete lives. The special concern with poverty applies to people who *are* poor, not to those who used to be poor but are now living in a reasonable degree of comfort. For example, it would apply to many African Americans living in inner-city neighborhoods. The same neighborhoods sometimes contain convenience stores owned by Asian Americans. In some cases the store owners will be recent immigrants. They might have suffered greatly in their countries of origin, living under extreme poverty and victimized by political oppression. But despite the harsh past, they are now living comfortably, and they can expect even better lives for their children. If we think in terms of complete lives, their lifetimes might count as being even worse than the complete life of an unemployed African

American single mother. Nevertheless, the special concern with poverty applies to the African American who is living in poverty, not to the Asian American. It provides a reason for a policy that will improve the lives of African Americans over one that would help the Asian- Americans, even if for some reason the second policy might actually bring about a greater good.

These ideas can be applied to the elderly. Some of the elderly are among the worst off. In virtue of that, benefits for them will have a special significance. What matters in determining this kind of priority is the current state of their lives. So the claim to priority remains in place even if they were much better off in the past and even if their complete lives are better than the predicted complete lives of younger people who are asked to help them (but it must compete with a claim of priority on behalf of the younger people that depends on lifetimes). The claim to priority remains in place even if it will be difficult to help them, and the resources in question would generate larger benefits if they were given to younger people.

The case of poverty is useful for testing another view of the application of priority to people at particular times. Sometimes people suspect that the claim that it is especially urgent to help badly off people among the elderly, even if their complete lives do not count as deprived, seems plausible only because the happiness that they experienced was in the past. The intuition behind the conclusion does not support a time-neutral application of priority to temporal stages in lives, it supports a view that treats past happiness or misery as unimportant and focuses only on the present and the future.

We know that, while some people live in poverty throughout their lives, others move into and out of that condition. A Canadian study suggests that 50 percent of the people who are now living below the poverty line will have escaped poverty within a year. So we can ask whether we would give the same importance to improving the current condition of the lives of people who are living in poverty if the happier condition is in their future rather than in the past. I think we still would feel this concern. In thinking about the question, we should remember that this example will also involve concerns about lifetimes. If we are not inclined to draw this conclusion, it might be because we are thinking in terms of lifetimes or because we think the official poverty line does not represent an important dividing line for awarding priority.

If we understand the moral claims of the elderly in the way I have suggested and if we interpret the goal of social security in the same way, it is striking that the claim of the elderly does not depend on their being old as such and it does not depend on their being in a special and distinctive stage of a human life. It is explained by the absolute condition of the current stage of their lives, and because of this, their claim must compete against the claims of others, for example inner-city dwellers living in poverty, that have essentially the same basis. This is not to deny that there might be other reasons—for example, gratitude for past contributions that they have made—that would also support helping the elderly.

Some writers reject any version of the priority view because they think it cannot be coherently stated.[1] This argument challenges both priority applied to lifetimes as well as to people at particular times. To make sense of priority, we must be able to distinguish between the size of a gain in well-being and the value attributed to that gain. This is necessary because the priority view holds that two equal-sized gains of well-being can have

---

1. This objection was suggested to me from comments made by John Broome. He is not responsible for what I have written.

different amounts of value, depending on the level of well-being of the person who experiences the gains. The argument claims that this distinction cannot be made, contending that the notion of well-being is itself an evaluative concept. When we speak of a certain amount of well-being, we are not making a straightforward factual claim, like the claim that a drawer contains a certain number of marbles. Instead, we are making a claim about value and specifying a certain amount of value. Identifying it as being a gain of well-being of a certain size is already determining how much value it has. So there is no room left for the priority view to say that the gain has more value because it is experienced by someone badly off. That amounts to saying that the gain has more value than it actually has.

I think the criticism can be answered. I am not convinced that well-being is an evaluative concept in the sense the argument requires. Of course we value well-being, and we think that it counts as a good, but I am not sure that someone who denied that well-being was good would be saying something absurd. I think he would be wrong, but the claim that well-being is good might be a substantive moral judgment.

However, perhaps I am wrong. Perhaps we cannot call something well-being and at the same time deny that it is good or has value. In that case, I would reformulate the priority view by talking about the constituents of well-being rather than well-being itself. I think that the states and activities that are the constituents of well-being could not plausibly be claimed to be evaluative concepts. We could make the distinctive claims that the priority view posits about those constituents rather than about well-being. For example, knowledge might be one constituent of well-being according to a perfectionist view of the concept. But knowledge is not an evaluative concept in the sense the criticism requires.

We could coherently say that it would be better to increase the understanding of someone with little knowledge by a small amount rather than to increase the understanding of someone who knows a great deal by a larger amount. This is a particularized version of the priority view, and we could do the same in the case of many other possible constituents of well-being.

5.2 APPLYING PRIORITY TO TEMPORAL PARTS OF LIVES

When we apply priority to a temporal part of a life, I call this the time-specific priority view. But should we apply priority to a temporal part of a life? Do we really think that a mere temporal stage in a life, as opposed to a complete lifetime, can be the basis of a claim of priority?

One test case is a person who lives happily until old age and then falls into misfortune. The biblical story of Job (used by Temkin for a different purpose) is an example. Job is introduced in this way: "His substance also was seven thousand sheep, and three thousand camels, and five hundred yoke of oxen, and five hundred she asses, and a very great household; so that this man was the greatest of all the men of the east" (1:3). Despite his prosperity, we are expected to empathize with the extreme suffering on Job's part that follows. After Job has repaired his relationship with God, we are told, "Then came there unto him all his brethren, and all his sisters, and all they that had been of his acquaintance before, and did eat bread with him in his house, and they bemoaned him, and comforted him over all the evil that the Lord had brought upon him: every man also gave him a piece of money, and every one an earring of gold" (42:11). This somewhat belated generosity by his relatives and neighbors would be odd if they were thinking in terms of lifetimes rather than the current phase of Job's life. I am sure there were many men with worse complete lives than Job. Unfortunately, it is difficult to tell whether the story of Job counts as an example of suffering during old age, since we are also told that he lived for another 140 years after his period of tribulation (42:16).

When applied to temporal stages of lives or to people at particular times, the priority view escapes what I consider to be the most compelling objections against the simultaneous segments view about equality.

To begin with, a specific example will provide a different kind of reason to think that our judgments about distribution between the temporal stages of lives are explained by priority rather than equality. Suppose that during a temporal stages T1 A and B both have a level of well-being of 1, while during T2 A is at 5 while B is at 4. Suppose also that we can award one extra unit of well-being to B, and the unit can be added either during T1 or T2. Either way, adding the unit creates equality between the complete lives of A and B. If the unit is added during T2, it will also create simultaneous segments equality between A and B. If it is added during T1, it will increase simultaneous segments inequality, but it will go to someone who is currently badly off. The concern for simultaneous segments equality tells us to add the unit during T2. This conclusion is reached because the simultaneous segments view does not just indicate who should be helped within a given time period (neither A nor B in T1, B in T2), it applies across time periods to show which person it is the most important to help (B in T2 rather than A or B during T1). However, I think most of us would choose to help B during T1, assuming that the level of well-being represented by 1 is a life of low absolute quality. This is evidence that our conclusion is based on priority, not equality.

In the case of priority as opposed to equality, it is relatively easy to decide how to apply the value to people at particular times. There is no reason to suppose that the view should take different forms, corresponding to the three different views about equality. The fundamental idea is that the value of a gain in well-being for a given person depends on the level of well-being of that person when the gain is experienced. We can say exactly the same thing about any other gains for any other people at any other times. The idea applies to all people at all times in precisely the same way. So when we are applying the idea of priority to decide who to help, there is no reason to restrict our thinking to the condition of other people at the same time or to people who are in the same temporal stage of life. In deciding who should receive priority, we should simply consider all people at all times.

This proposal will seem to clash with what I have said about applying equality to life stages in chapter 4. I am suggesting that priority should be applied across all times, while earlier I claimed that equality can only be plausibly applied to the simultaneous stages of lives. There are fundamental differences between the values of equality and priority, but they are also closely related in many ways. As a result, they tend to reach the same conclusions about many, but not all, examples although they draw those conclusions for different reasons. So we may find it difficult to decide whether an egalitarian conclusion about a particular example is best understood in terms of priority or in terms of equality.

I am committed to the view that the application of priority to all temporal stages of lives across time is intuitively persuasive. However, we would reach the same conclusions in most of the relevant cases if we were instead to apply the value of equality in the same way. So how can it be reasonable to claim, as I did in chapter 4, that the only intuitively persuasive way of applying equality to life stages is the simultaneous segments view? Apparently the same examples, interpreted in a different way, should count as intuitively persuasive applications of equality.

One point to make in reply is that, if we accept this reasoning and drop the condition of simultaneity when applying equality to temporal parts of lives, we will not be led to the corresponding segments view, a view that some people are inclined to accept in any case. We will be led to the total segments view, the true equivalent in the case of equality to my way of applying priority. This would require finding something objectionable in an inequality between the youth of one person and the middle age of someone else, even when those two life stages are not simultaneous and there is no inequality between their lifetimes. I find this counterintuitive in the extreme. Still, perhaps some people might be willing to accept the total segments view and draw this conclusion.

The best way of explaining how there can be a difference between equality and priority is to return to the fundamental difference between the two values: Equality is a relative value while priority is an absolute value. Judgments about equality are made about relations between different lives (unless we have decided to extend the application of the value and apply it to different temporal stages of the same life—but this would still be a relative or comparative application of the value), while at the most fundamental level, judgments of priority are made about a single life. Since equality is an essentially comparative value, whenever we apply it, the question always arises of which comparisons are the relevant and morally important ones. Which items or subjects are such that a claim to equality holds between them?

Suppose that we are considering applying equality between the temporal stages of different lives. I think it seems to us at least initially that the simultaneous temporal stages of different lives are relevant subjects of comparison, but not any two stages in different lives (or, for that matter, the different temporal stages of the same life). So this is where we will think a claim to equality holds. Our intuition is that simultaneity is needed to make two life stages in different lives sufficiently salient to each other for us to judge that there should be equality between them. This application of the comparative value seems important and morally relevant while the other applications do not.

However, none of this reasoning applies to the case of priority. It is not a relative or comparative value at all. So when we consider applying it to temporal stages of lives, we are not faced with the question of which stages of which lives are relevant to the comparisons being made. There is no reason not to simply apply the value to all stages of all lives. The claim that priority makes about well-being and value applies to every life. Consequently, simultaneity is irrelevant. Priority depends on the absolute condition of lives or stages of lives, not on relations between them. A priority judgment made about life stages, whether they are simultaneous or not, is just a judgment about which life stage it is more important to improve. We are responding to this difference between the two values when we find the total segments view about equality intuitively implausible while we nevertheless find the unrestricted application of priority to temporal stages of lives intuitively plausible.

To be clear, my view is that, in many cases, there will be a strong case for redistribution between nonsimultaneous stages of different lives. For example, we might tax younger people now to create resources that will be devoted to the elderly at some future time. These judgments are best explained by priority, not by the total segments view of equality.

Since priority is concerned with improving the absolute condition of the badly off, not with removing the inequality that exists

PRIORITY

between those people and others, everyone would not be required
to suffer more to prevent inequality at a particular time. The priority view, whether it is concerned with complete lifetimes or
with temporal parts of lives, rejects leveling down as a matter of
principle.

Also, the priority view, unlike the simultaneous segments view
about equality, can easily handle cases of momentary suffering. If
two people experience suffering that only lasts for a moment, it
does not seem unreasonable to give at least some priority to helping the one whose suffering is the more intense. Agonizing pain
is morally important even if it only lasts for a moment, and the
view can recognize its importance. But at the same time, if a less
intense pain lasts longer than the extreme pain, the priority view
has the resources to draw the conclusion that ending the milder
pain might outweigh ending the more intense suffering. The value
of escaping three hours of steady persistent pain might be greater
than the value of escaping an agonizing but momentary pain.
Finally, the priority view does not give any importance to simultaneity as such. If we compare the values of gains received by two
different people by applying priority to particular times or to temporal stages in lives, we get the same answer whether the gains are
simultaneous or not. So unlike the simultaneous segments view,
the priority does not have to explain and justify giving intrinsic
moral importance to facts about time.

5.3 ANSWERING OBJECTIONS TO THE
TIME-SPECIFIC PRIORITY VIEW

The priority view applied to people at particular times would
answer the objection based on compensation over time in a

different way from the view that applies equality to people at times. Consider this example:

	T1	T2	T3
A	8	2	
B		8	2

How could there be a case for transferring resources from B to A during T2? B is badly off during T2, but he is fully compensated for this by his higher level of welfare during T1.

The equality view (more specifically, the simultaneous segments view) counters by detaching the concern for equality from facts about the absolute quality of lives as opposed to facts about relations between lives. Redistribution during T2 would reduce the simultaneous inequality between the two lives during T2. It would change the relationship between the lives during that time period, in a way that the simultaneous segments view sees as an improvement. This truth about the redistribution is not altered by A's high level of welfare during T1.

The priority view would reply to the objection in a different way. In one sense, A might not be fully compensated for his low quality of life in T2 by his higher quality of life in T1. That is because the extra welfare he enjoys during T1 might not be as important or significant as the benefits he might have received during T2 when he is badly off. According to the priority view, if a unit of well-being were transferred from B to A during T2, the loss to B might not be as important as the gain for A. The simplest and most plausible version of the priority view would reach the same conclusion about transferring a unit of well-being from A during T1 to A during T2, if that transfer were possible. According to the priority view, both transfers would bring about a genuine improvement in the quality of peoples' lives—the first transfer would trade a less important loss for B for a more important gain for A, while the second transfer would benefit A overall—not merely change the relations between lives. So the priority view can answer the objection without detaching our concern from the absolute quality of the lives.

This seems to be an advantage for the priority view. Some egalitarians care about equality in the way that I have appealed to in defending the simultaneous segments view against the objections from compensation and from prudence. But nonegalitarians are suspicious of this way of caring about equality, and even some egalitarians would prefer to rest the concern for equality on some other ground. In the case of leveling down, some egalitarians are willing to accept views that have that result while others struggle to find a formulation of an egalitarian theory that will avoid such a result. Without attempting to resolve these disagreements, it is worth pointing out that a view based on priority completely avoids both problematic features.

However, when it comes to the objection about choice and responsibility, the priority view might seem to be less persuasive than the simultaneous segments view. In the case of equality, many egalitarians believe that if the inequality results from the unconstrained choices of the people who are worse off under the inequality, or is in some other way their responsibility, then the inequality is not objectionable. If we apply equality to temporal parts of lives we can, if we choose, make the same claim about that kind of inequality. This enables us to apply equality to people at times and at the same time hold them responsible for past choices that produced the inequality.

In the case of priority, a difficulty is created by the explanation of why priority should be applied to people at times, which appealed to the way that we value well-being. Its central claim was that a benefit has special value if it is received by someone who is badly off, just because that person is badly off. If this claim really is a consequence of the way we value well-being, then a benefit will possess that special value if it is received by anyone who is badly off. Even if a person is wholly responsible for her own misery, a benefit for her will have the special value that I associate with priority.

The worry is that priority applied to people at times will not be able to account for our ideas about responsibility. Suppose two people are equally very badly off. One bears the responsibility for her situation, the other does not. The priority view does not give us a reason to help the second person rather than the first. A benefit received by either person would have special value and the same amount of value, provided the benefits are also equal in size. This is a conclusion that many people would be reluctant to accept.

However, this difficulty is not fundamental. If we explain priority in the way I have suggested, we cannot deny that a benefit received by someone badly off has special value even if she is responsible for her own suffering. Nevertheless, we might be able to preserve our ideas about responsibility by making adjustments to other aspects of our moral view. Instead of trying to include responsibility in the egalitarian value, which is essentially what those egalitarians do who make the wrongness of inequality depend on responsibility, we might treat responsibility as an independent value with which the egalitarian value must compete. Priority is concerned with value that depends on the well-being experienced by people, but that is not the only kind of value that generates moral reasons relevant to deciding what it would be best to do. With respect to the example, we might say that, although a benefit for either person would have the same value when considered as increases of well-being, it is also true that the second deserves to be helped in a way that the first person does not, where desert is a value independent of priority, and that is why we should help her. Or we might say there is value in holding people responsible for their choices, a value that does not depend on egalitarian priority and is not directly related to the value of well-being but that counts against helping the first person. Some such strategy might disarm the objection.

The priority view also avoids another serious concern about the simultaneous segments view, the problem of deciding what the temporal scope of egalitarian principles should be—what temporal unit we should use instead of a complete lifetime. In the case of equality, we seemed forced to choose between an arbitrarily specified stretch of time—arbitrary because any such stretch might contain within itself simultaneous inequality that our principle could not take into account—or making the temporal scope a mere moment, a designation that also seemed to lead to implausibility.

Initially, the priority view seemingly faces exactly the same problem. Suppose that we are considering applying the value of priority to an individual's old age, because that person is badly off. There may be a difference between his level of well-being in his old age as a whole and his well-being during some shorter temporal stretch during his old age when he would actually receive the benefits provided. So there is a question about which temporal unit we should use in the application of priority—his old age as a whole or that shorter period of time within his old age. The two choices can lead to different results, since the degree of priority that he should receive will depend on what we take to be his level of well-being, which depends on which temporal unit we use.

This problem can be resolved in the case of priority.[2] The priority view does not have difficulty in addressing the case of intense

---

2. For the purpose of answering the objection, I will assume that we can make sense of a person having a certain level of well-being at a particular time. Some will reject that

105

suffering that lasts for only a moment. This suggests that we can regard fundamental priority judgments as dealing with people at particular times, at least to the extent that our notion of well-being is precise enough to allow us to make judgments about the well-being of people at particular times. Priority judgments that deal with larger intervals of time can be regarded as analyzable into priority judgments about particular times. In the case of equality, this reduction led to implausible consequences because of special features of the value of equality. There is no reason to think the same will happen in the case of priority.

I am supposing that we can specify a person's level of well-being at a particular time. It seems wrong to claim that we cannot make sense of the thought that person A's level of well-being at a particular time T1 is higher than person B's level of well-being at the same time. Given the nature of well-being, there may be cases in which it might not be possible to answer the question or in which the answer we can give might not be determinate enough to allow us to apply priority. In any case, this seems to be a problem that we would face in giving a philosophical account of well-being. If the best account of well-being only partially solves the problem, that would not be a reason to reject in principle the application of priority to people at particular times. Even if I am wrong and we can only sensibly talk about a person's level of well-being with reference to an extended interval of time, I think that the priority view would still be able to assess a gain by using the level of well-being over the shortest interval that included the gain.

I will briefly comment on some reasons that might be offered for thinking that there is a difficulty of principle in talking about well-being at a specific time. Nagel suggests that the goods that

assumption, but the particular objection I am trying to answer does not depend on it being impossible to identify a person's level of well-being at a specific time.

egalitarianism is especially concerned with are "aspects of the individual's life taken as a whole: health, nourishment, freedom, work, education, self-respect, affection, pleasure."[3] Most of these goods will extend over long temporal stretches of the person's life. Work, for example, might include many years of preparation and then the successful execution of worthwhile projects.

Such a career can be an important constituent of the person's well-being, but it might seem foolish to even attempt to say how much well-being resulted from one typical week of work.

Here I appeal to Thomas Hurka's treatment of a similar question.[4] If there is enough unity in the career of the person in question, it is legitimate to assign values to mundane short-term activities because they are contributing parts of a successful, long-term project. How much value we assign to a particular part may be somewhat arbitrary, but we do not have to treat the career as an undifferentiated whole without being able to say anything about the importance of the choices and actions that make up the career.

Some writers think there can be kinds of well-being that cannot be assigned any temporal location inside our lives, whether at a particular time or during an extended interval. For example, David Velleman believes there can be "structural goods" which make our lives better without increasing our well-being at any specific time.[5] One of his examples is that a life is better if success follows failure rather than having failure follow success. We may not

3. Nagel, "Equality," 117.
4. Thomas Hurka, *Perfectionism* (Oxford: Oxford University Press, 1993, 69–70, 110–11, 118–19). Hurka is explicitly concerned with perfectionist goods, but I think we can adopt a similar view about well-being. He would object to this extension because he thinks that the notion of well-being should be replaced by the more traditional notion of intrinsic goods.
5. David Velleman, "Well-Being and Time" *Pacific Philosophical Quarterly* 72, no.1, 1991, 48–77.

JUSTICE BETWEEN THE YOUNG AND THE OLD

be convinced by his case, but suppose we agree. If the gain does not have a temporal location, then we cannot say what the person's level of well-being is when the gain is received, so we cannot apply the priority view concerned with temporal parts of lives. In this case I would say that this kind of well-being is not relevant to priority concerned with particular times, but it should be taken into account in priority judgments dealing with lifetimes.

There is another way of trying to explain why the priority view has an important advantage over the equality view with respect to the issue of specifying the temporal scope of its principle. In certain formal respects, the priority view resembles utilitarianism. The difference between the two views is that, while utilitarianism assigns a value to a gain in well-being that is simply proportional to the size of the gain, the priority view also weights the value of the gain according to the overall level of welfare of the person who experiences it, where the relevant level of welfare is the person's well-being when the gain is received. So if utilitarianism were to assign, for example, a specific value to an increase of two units of well-being, the priority view might well assign more value to that gain if it was experienced by someone at a low level of well-being.

Suppose someone were to suggest that utilitarianism poses a problem in choosing a temporal unit for the application of its principle, a problem that is analogous to the problem that I have discussed in the case of the equality view. Should it use the temporal unit of a mere moment, or should its principles be applied at the level of longer intervals of time? Will the view not reach different conclusions depending on which temporal unit is chosen?

No one would regard this as a real problem for utilitarianism. The utilitarian view will register the size of gains and losses in terms of well-being, assign values to them, and then aggregate the values and draw its conclusion. Because this procedure is used, the view will reach the same conclusion irrespective of which temporal unit it employs. Or we might say that, given the nature of the utilitarian view, there is no need to choose a temporal unit—it does not do any work in reaching the conclusion. If the case includes well-being that is assigned to particular individuals at particular moments, then the view takes that well-being into account. If there is a portion of well-being that cannot be assigned to people at particular times, then the view would have to take that well-being into account as well, which does not create a dilemma about choosing a temporal unit.

The priority view sets to work assessing outcomes in exactly the same way as utilitarianism, except that it weighs the values of the gains and losses according to the levels of the welfare of the people who receive them. The view differs from utilitarianism in the values it assigns to those gains and losses but not in how it uses the values to evaluate outcomes and draw its conclusions. If utilitarianism does not face a problem about assigning a temporal scope to its principle, neither does the priority view. Like utilitarianism, it may have to deal with complicated questions about whether all of the well-being that matters can be assigned to particular people at particular moments, but that is not the same as the issue of choosing a temporal unit. For the priority view, the so-called temporal unit does not play the same role or have the same importance as in the case of the equality view. In the case of equality, the temporal unit sets the boundaries within which we should look for equality, and that will importantly affect the conclusions to which the view leads. In the case of priority, there is no similar role for the temporal unit to play.

The comparison with utilitarianism may make some suspect that the judgments I am trying to explain can be satisfactorily accounted for by a utilitarian view. Perhaps we should help a suffering elderly person rather than his younger neighbor even though it is the younger person who will have the worse complete life, but this is simply because we will be able to help the older person more precisely because his current misery is so pronounced. There is no need to invoke the notion of priority. My answer would appeal to the extreme difficulty of helping many categories of suffering people among the elderly. Given the depth of their problems, it is much more realistic to think that we will be able to help them less. If we still feel that we should do what we can for them, the notion of priority seems to be an essential part of the explanation.

5.4 THE CASE FOR THE TIME-SPECIFIC PRIORITY VIEW

I have given a number of reasons why the application of priority to temporal parts of lives is more persuasive than the parallel application of equality. The reasons are specifically concerned with how we think about temporal parts of lives; they are not general reasons for thinking that priority is a more defensible value than equality that would also apply to egalitarian concerns focused on lifetimes. The reasons will not persuade everyone who is sympathetic to caring about parts of lives for their own sake to adopt priority, but I think that together they make a persuasive case.[6]

Perhaps the strongest consideration is the simplicity of the priority view concerned with particular times, when it is compared

---

6. I have not tried to explain how the priority view would respond to the objection based on prudence or how it would answer the objection that applying priority to a temporal part of a life means denying that a lifetime is a morally important unit. I will discuss each of these matters in chapter 6.

to the simultaneous segments view about equality (or, for that matter, when it is compared to the two other ways of applying equality to parts of lives). Simplicity is not a guarantee of truth, but the priority view is much easier to state and understand than the alternatives dealing with equality. No doubt some will find the view unconvincing or mistaken, but I think that is because they object to applying egalitarian values to temporal parts of lives. If they are egalitarians, they agree with Nagel's complete lives view. In subsequent chapters, I will discuss both priority and equality with respect to other issues, but I think that we should work with the value of priority.

As in the case of equality, if we accept egalitarian priority as a value, we should apply it both to lifetimes and to people at particular times. The person whose complete life is worst has a claim to receive a benefit, even if it would be experienced at a time when he was faring reasonably well. The person who would be worst off at the time the benefit is received has a competing claim to be given priority.[7]

A different distributive choice shows that we should give some weight to priority applied to lifetimes. Suppose that two people face imminent death without an organ transplant, and there is only one available organ that can be used. The first person is 30 years old, while the second is 75. The first person has some claim to receive the organ. This is not to say that the younger person receiving the organ must be the best choice. Perhaps there could be reasons of another sort that would outweigh this reason for

---

7. Kappel believes that priority should not be applied to lifetimes. He appeals to cases in which we would help the person who is suffering the most now rather than the person who has suffered most throughout her life as a whole. The example is persuasive, and it is an effective way of showing that priority is not always based on lifetimes. But these examples only show that we apply priority to people at particular times as well as to lifetimes, not that we do not apply priority to lifetimes.

awarding the organ to him. Still, he has a claim that must be taken into account even if we decide in the end that it is outweighed, and the claim depends on the fact that his life will be so much shorter than that of the other candidate if he is allowed to die at 30. In this example, the reason for giving a kind of priority to him can only be understood by thinking about lifetimes—it disappears if we only consider the current condition of the two lives.

Frances Kamm discusses these choices.[8] Her view is close to the priority view. She would say that the 75-year-old person has a claim to the organ based on what she calls need. Her notion of need corresponds to priority applied to lifetimes. Suppose that the 30-year-old will die in one year if he does not receive the organ, while the 75-year-old would live for two more years without the transplant. Kamm would say that the 30-year-old has a claim to the organ based on what she calls "urgency (time)." Her notion of urgency with respect to time is like priority applied to people at times. However, Kamm understands her notion in a way that can give intrinsic importance to facts about timing. The deciding factor for her in this example is how soon the person will die if he does not receive the organ. Another notion she calls "urgency (condition)" is much like priority applied to people at times. It holds that the person whose level of well-being is the lowest now—not the person with the lowest lifetime well-being—can have a claim to be given a treatment, even if the treatment would benefit the other person more. Kamm thinks that, in these examples, we can have a special concern with the present as such. She says our judgments reflect the "moral pressure of the here and now." I disagree. I think these judgments can be accounted for by a time-neutral understanding of priority.

8. *Intricate Ethics* (New York: Oxford University Press, 2007, 37–40).

I have suggested that the principles of justice governing synchronic distribution between people of different ages are best understood as an application of the value of equality, or the value of giving priority to the interests of the worst off, to temporal parts of lives.[9] One proposal is that a deep inequality between a temporal part of one life and a simultaneous temporal part of another life is important for its own sake, even if there is no inequality between the complete lives of the people in question. The other proposal is that, if a person is very badly off during a temporal part of her life, benefits that she might receive during that period should be given priority over benefits that other people would receive when they were not badly off, even if her complete life is not worse than the complete lives of the other people. My view is that we should give weight to these concerns in addition to concerns about lifetimes, not that they should replace concerns about lifetimes.

There is a significant difference between equality and priority over the issue of temporal units. In the case of equality, it is difficult to convince ourselves that it needs to be applied to parts of lives as well as to lifetimes, while for priority the case for applying it to parts of lives seems to be as strong, if not stronger, than the case for applying it to lifetimes. The difference is not simply explained by the fact that equality is essentially comparative and priority is

9. It would be puzzling if equality or priority could be applied to stages in lives but it was obviously unreasonable to do this with other values concerned with justice. Desert is a good comparison because of the strong parallels between theories of desert and theories of equality. In chapter 1, I mentioned W. D. Ross's theory of desert. He believes that pleasure should be distributed in accordance with virtue, and he insists that the principle of desert should consider lifetimes. However, Ross's view can be resisted. Suppose an idealistic reformer succeeds, at the cost of great personal unhappiness, in overthrowing a corrupt regime. Once in power, he becomes as cynical and oppressive as the dictator he replaced. Is it just if he experiences great happiness as a tyrant so that his lifetime happiness will match his lifetime virtue? Perhaps we want virtuous people to be happy when they are virtuous.

not. The source of the difference is that this application of equality requires giving a certain kind of importance to facts about timing, while doing so is not necessary in applying priority.

Some people may feel that the priority view, even if it expresses a valid moral reason, should not be understood as part of a theory of justice. In their view, justice must be a relative or comparative moral notion. Justice is concerned with how people fare relatively to others, and an injustice will be a matter of some people doing significantly better than others at times when this difference cannot be given the appropriate kind of justification. If the proponents of this view are right, equality but not priority can be a value connected with justice. So they would think that, even if we apply priority to temporal parts of lives in the way that I have described and so draw the corresponding conclusions about helping people of different ages, these ideas should not be considered as revealing something about justice between the young and the old. On the other hand, the simultaneous segments view about equality, assuming that we find it intuitively persuasive and are not convinced by the objections against it, would be appropriately called a principle of justice between the young and the old.

I have not tried to answer this concern. It is tempting to consider it as essentially a semantic worry, but that may underestimate its importance. Without attempting to fully resolve this issue, the priority view applied to people at times might be the kind of principle that constrains the institution of social security in the way that people are thinking of when they debate about justice between the young and the old. The priority view is about who has the strongest claim to be helped (remembering that I am not saying that egalitarian priority is the only idea relevant to determining the strength of people's claims). When people are very badly off—and most of my examples and arguments are concerned with people in that condition—the claims based on priority are correspondingly strong. We might think that social institutions and governments are obliged to satisfy these claims, unless there are equally weighty reasons for not doing so, and at least in terms of ordinary language, meeting these claims might be described as a concern of justice. This point holds for views about complete lives as much as for the special case of priority applied to people at times. Some people will think that the reason for helping people who are the worst off is supplied by priority not equality, and they will see acting on the reason as a matter of social justice. The fact that, in less extreme cases, it would not ordinarily be considered an injustice to fail to help the person with the strongest claim based on priority does not show that those who subscribe to this view are making a mistake. Relatively minor inequalities would also not be classified as injustices, but that does not establish that equality is a value irrelevant to justice.

The ideas that I have used to explain justice between the young and the old do not apply exclusively to people of different ages, and they are not rooted in the characteristic differences between youth and old age as distinctive stages of life. They are about the moral significance of temporal parts of lives, a significance that is, to some extent, independent of the moral importance of complete lives. So they would also apply to exact contemporaries, for example to inequality between the simultaneous middle ages of different people.

The fact that the difference between age and youth is not part of the explanation of this moral concern at the deepest level is not a reason to reject the explanation. When we consider what the view requires in the case of synchronic distribution between age groups—for example, whether there should be strict equality between the young and the old, what kinds of resources the claims apply to—the characteristic differences between youth and age might be relevant to the answers.

If I am right, inequality between the young and the old is not more of an injustice than inequality between the temporal parts of the lives of people of the same age, inequality that might reflect class, race, or gender rather than age. It might seem puzzling that an institution, one of whose central purposes is specifically to help the elderly in need, should have become entrenched in many very different societies, when institutions that would address those other inequalities have not been so fortunate. Historical explanations of the success of social security appeal to many different factors. One is the way the institution combines its welfare goal with a savings goal that benefits (almost) everyone. The fact that most social security systems are contributory makes it easier for us to think that the recipients have earned their benefits. Old age is also arguably the stage in our lives when we might fall the furthest behind other people and experience the deepest distress without social assistance. The misery that people experience when they are old and unable to work is not likely to be regarded as their fault, a problem that they should be responsible for solving themselves, or a result of one of their own choices.

Egalitarian concerns dealing with temporal parts of lives can sometimes outweigh egalitarian concerns focused on lifetimes. This conclusion distinguishes my view from Daniels's theory in which the frame theory always takes precedence over the prudential life span account. However, some people might feel that this claim is both controversial and unnecessary. Why not be satisfied with a more modest view that held instead that, although concerns about temporal parts of lives matter for their own sake, they are always outweighed by fairness at the level of lifetimes? This view would still be distinct from the prudential life span account because it reaches different conclusions about distribution over temporal parts of lives.

Nothing in the nature of priority (or, for that matter, equality—I am discussing this issue in terms of priority because, as I have argued in this chapter, I think priority is the most suitable egalitarian value to apply to temporal parts of lives) guarantees that lifetime considerations will outweigh considerations dealing with temporal parts of lives. A benefit added to a life that is of low quality assessed as a whole will have special value, as will a benefit received by someone who is currently badly off. Which has more value will depend on the size of the benefit and the degree of priority, and I see no reason why the result must be that the first benefit is more important. In addition, sometimes it seems intuitively persuasive to choose the benefit for someone who is badly off at a particular time. Relevant cases are the example of the African Americans and the Asian American shopkeepers, the story of Job, and the comparison between the people in the condominiums and the people in the nursing home in chapter 1.

Chapter 6

Personal Identity and Prudence

6.1 PERSONAL IDENTITY AND EGALITARIANISM

I have explained one important part of justice between age groups by supposing that the values of equality and priority can legitimately be applied to temporal stages in lives as well as to complete lives or lifetimes. However, some will think that I am ignoring an indispensable, deeper explanation of the conclusions that I have drawn.

It has been suggested—by philosophers but also by writers and some religious thinkers—that what we ordinarily think of as a temporally complete and unified human life involves a serious weakening in the identity of the person whose life it is. This thought might be provoked by an appreciation of the extent and the significance of the physical and psychological changes a person undergoes over time as her life progresses from the cradle to the grave. Or it might be the result of philosophical reflection on the nature of personal identity over time. Whatever its source, it implies that, in my old age, I will not be the same person that I now am. The meaning and strength of this claim can vary depending on the particular view of personal identity that prompts it.

If we think about personal identity in this way, it is easy to explain why we should have independent moral concerns focused on temporal parts of lives. Consider Nagel's argument about compensation across time inside a life, one of the reasons for restricting principles of justice to the temporal scope of lifetimes. On such an understanding of personal identity Nagel's argument fails. Compensation, in Nagel's sense of the term, presupposes personal identity. If my elderly self virtually counts as a different person, I cannot be compensated for my misfortunes with benefits that he will receive. My current level of well-being or welfare should be irrelevant to determining what would be fair for him, and vice versa.

This view of personal identity would also explain why the traditional view of prudence should not be the model for understanding justice between age groups. Exercising prudence involves determining what will make my life go best as a whole, considering that life from its beginning to its end. Yet with this view of personal identity, when I think about old age, or at least extreme old age, I may no longer be thinking about my life in the sense that matters for rationality and morality. The prudential concern must be restricted by the limits imposed by the correct account of personal identity through time. These limits may not coincide with the birth of a person in the ordinary sense and what we ordinarily think of as that same person's death.

This chapter will first be concerned with the claim that some revisionist way of understanding personal identity is needed for us to apply equality and priority to parts of lives. If we are to give priority to improving the quality of a person's life during some particular stage of it, or if we are to have a genuine concern about inequality between that stage and some contemporaneous stage in another life, we must be thinking about that particular life stage in isolation from the complete life to which it belongs. It will only make sense to apply moral values to the life stage itself outside the context of the complete life if the person during that stage is somehow distinct from the person at other times during his or her life. The new way of understanding personal identity would establish the necessary distinctness. If old age were merely, as common sense supposes, a passing phase in the life of one and the same person who persists through every temporal stage of the life, we might think that it is enough to view that life as a whole in considering fairness. So applying the value to the stage itself rather than to the life as a whole requires thinking about life stages in a special way.

The suggestion is that the moral revisionism of applying values to temporal stages of lives requires support from metaphysical revisionism about the identity of the person whose life it is. The view of personal identity provides a reason for the conclusion that we should have independent moral concerns with temporal stages of lives. I argue against this view: Applying egalitarian values to temporal parts of lives does not require support from a theory of personal identity. The arguments in this discussion will also lead to a new way of understanding prudential rationality.

In chapters 4 and 5, I applied egalitarian values to stages in lives, which helps to explain how egalitarianism connects with the subject of this chapter.

Some egalitarians contend that egalitarianism is an expression of a distinctive way of weighing the gains and losses of different people. They think it is more reasonable than the utilitarian way of assessing such gains and losses. According to their view, egalitarianism depends on the existence of a contrast between interpersonal and intrapersonal choices.

Within a life we should simply choose the greatest possible surplus of benefits over harms, irrespective of how that well-being will be spread across a lifetime. A greater benefit experienced at one time in the life can outweigh a lesser harm experienced at some other moment in the life. However, when different people are involved, then egalitarian distributional constraints need to be taken into account. The constraints express the independent moral importance of individuals. They matter in cases in which different people are concerned. They are the appropriate moral response to the so-called separateness of persons.

However, the constraints do not apply in the case of a single person; the values of equality and priority are restricted to interpersonal choices and cannot be applied to intrapersonal choices.[1] In chapters 4 and 5, I suggested that egalitarian values could be applied to temporal parts of different lives, but I did not suggest that they could be applied inside a single life.

Given these ideas, we would need to have a special reason in order to apply egalitarian values intrapersonally, but a particular view of personal identity could provide a justification. According to some accounts of identity, intrapersonal choices are much more like interpersonal choices than we think. There is a similarity between the relationship between a person at two different times and the relationship between two different people. Some ways of thinking about identity might allow us to find the separateness of persons—or some weaker analogue to it—inside one life. The appeal to such a view will bring with it the intrapersonal application of egalitarian values.

I will not argue for or against revisionist philosophical accounts of personal identity, but I will argue that they are neither necessary nor helpful in understanding justice.

---

1. John Rawls makes this suggestion in *A Theory of Justice*, 27–28), and Thomas Nagel proposes a similar idea in *The Possibility of Altruism* (Oxford: Clarendon Press, 1970, 142). I criticized this explanation of egalitarianism in "Egalitarianism and the Separateness of Persons," *Canadian Journal of Philosophy* 18, 1988, 205–26.

6.2 THE APPEAL TO IDENTITY

The simplest revisionist view of personal identity replaces the idea of a single, self-identical person who persists through all of the different temporal stages of a lifetime with the notion of a series of closely related but numerically distinct selves that succeed one another during an ordinary life. Richard Posner appeals to this view in discussing justice and social security.[2] He comments: "The change in the individual between youth and old age is so profound that it becomes plausible to imagine the individual's young and old selves as different persons, 'time-sharing' the same body" (95). This view understands the concept of replacement in a literal way. There is no continuing person, only the series of selves. The selves are related in important ways—much more so than selves that belong to different lives—but the relationship among them is not identity.

Posner does not use what he calls "multiple selves analysis" to draw specific conclusions about fairness between age groups. He is unwilling to endorse any particular view of justice, but his view makes the distribution between my younger self and my elder self equivalent to a distribution between different people. He states that this view rules out the possibility of determining my fair share of resources in old age by appealing to a prudential choice made when I am young. If the two selves can be viewed as two different people, there is no reason to permit the preferences of my young self to determine the fate of my older self (98). Posner thinks that the striking differences in preferences and values that are typically found between a person at the age of 20 and that person at the age of 80 support his case for thinking of the life as being lived by different selves.

2. See especially pp. 263–64, 281–82, and 293.

His view fits my characterization of the supposed link between personal identity and justice between age groups. He believes that there are concerns of justice that are not focused on complete lifetimes and criticizes views that appeal to rational prudence in settling distribution between the young and the old. He applies justice to temporal stages of lives interpersonally and intrapersonally.

Posner's view is extreme. Changes in preferences seem insufficient to justify speaking of two different selves. Parfit proposes a more complex view of personal identity that does not require a literal metaphysics of selves.[3] He claims that personal identity through time consists of relations of psychological and physical continuity and connectedness that hold between a person's states at the various times in her life. My concern is not with the issue of personal identity itself, so I will not attempt to state this "complex" or "reductionist" view. Parfit appeals to many different kinds of psychological and physical continuity, so his view has a stronger basis than that of Posner.

Parfit sketches some of the view's implications for distributive justice, without referring to age. He believes that, if we think about identity in this way, we will be more likely to apply such values as equality and priority to the temporal parts of different peoples' lives and, in a parallel way, to the different temporal parts of the same life. This is a matter of changing the temporal scope of distributive principles. However, he also believes his theory of identity might incline us to give less weight or importance to the distributive constraints that the two values represent.[4] Parfit

---

3. Derek Parfit, *Reasons and Persons* (Oxford: Oxford University Press, 1984, 339–445); see also "Comments" *Ethics* 96, 1986, 832–72, especially pp. 869–72.

4. However, there will only be a real change in our beliefs if we make certain assumptions. The first is that our current beliefs center the moral importance of the unity of human lives and the appropriateness of distributional constraints on personal identity as it is understood by the common sense view of personal identity, not on physical and

supposes that this view of identity also leads us to question the authority of prudential rationality as it is ordinarily understood. Parfit draws one strong conclusion. He claims that the application of certain moral notions throughout a lifetime presupposes that personal identity over time should be what he calls a "further fact" distinct from relations of psychological and physical connectedness and continuity. He then argues that there is no such further fact to personal identity.[5] This conclusion undermines the application of notions of responsibility and desert across the temporal stages of a life. It also might motivate applying a requirement of equality inside a life, on the grounds that deprivations that one might experience early in life cannot be compensated for by benefits that one might receive at a later age. If this argument succeeds, it seems that we could not continue to apply equality and priority to complete lives.[6]

There is another way of using facts about psychological connections to support the moral conclusions I drew in chapter 4. Jeff

psychological relations. Unless our current beliefs take that form, there is no reason for them to change if we become convinced that only those relations exist and there is no personal identity as the simple view conceives it. Second, we must believe that personal identity can only have the kind of moral importance that we now attribute to it if it really is a further fact distinct from physical and psychological relations. Unless we have this belief, being persuaded to reject the simple view of personal identity and accept the complex view will not necessarily produce the other change Parfit describes. We might instead continue to think that personal identity is very important—perhaps just as important as we believed it to be when we accepted the simple view of its nature—and continue to think that its importance makes distributional constraints appropriate.

5. *Reasons and Persons*, 342–45.

6. A difficulty for the argument is that it must show that compensation across time requires the simple kind of personal identity rather than the complex view that Parfit thinks is the correct understanding of personal identity. Parfit tries to do this by considering cases—double brain transplant or "splitting" examples—in which he thinks there is no personal identity but there is the physical and psychological connectedness and continuity that Parfit uses to understand identity. He thinks that in these examples we would judge that responsibility and compensation are not transmitted across the split, so this shows that those moral notions require personal identity in the simple sense, not

McMahan suggests that the psychological relations of continuity and connectedness that hold inside a life over time can have moral importance for their own sake. The importance does not depend on the fact—if it is a fact—that the relations constitute personal identity. Consider a person who is miserable during old age, although he was happy when he was young. The view suggests that, if we help him now that he is old, it is because of the weakening of the relations holding between the earlier stages of his life and the present. The weaker relations made his past happiness less relevant to the question of how he should be treated now. He is not a different self or a borderline case of personal identity. Instead psychological changes such as the decay of his memory and alterations in his character (but not just the passage of time itself) mean that we should, to some extent, discount that past happiness when we are considering whether to help him now.

6.3 PROBLEMS WITH THE APPEAL TO PERSONAL IDENTITY

I will oppose all of these views. I do not agree that the ethical ideas explained in chapter 4 require support from a view about the nature of identity through time. Even if we accept the ordinary view of personal identity, we might think that equality and priority can be applied to parts of lives as well as to entire

the complex sense. However, we might not agree with this assessment of the examples. We might believe that there can be compensation for past misfortune across the split. Moreover, even if we judge the examples in the way Parfit supposes, that may only be because we now believe that there is a further fact to identity and we recognize that it cannot be present in the splitting cases. If we were convinced—perhaps by reading Parfit's arguments—that there is not and cannot be such a further fact to identity, we might change our conclusions about the examples. We might come to believe that there can be moral responsibility and compensation across the split, even if that is not what we believe now.

lifetimes. We can make better sense of these moral claims if we interpret them as being self-standing and independent of considerations about identity. The appeal to personal identity does not make the moral claims more reasonable and easier to accept, but makes it harder to find a general principle that can explain the conclusions that have the strongest intuitive appeal. McMahan's view is not concerned with identity itself, but I will argue that the weakening of psychological connections over time does not play an important role in explaining our judgments about temporal parts of lives.

In the case of priority, applying the value to people at times does not require support from theories about personal identity. The judgments that we make about the importance of benefiting people who are currently badly off are self-standing. On the surface they seem to be independent of views of personal identity. Why should we be obliged to withdraw those judgments if we were convinced of the truth of a simple, nonreductionist theory of personal identity?

The explanation of priority judgments about persons at particular times proposed in chapter 5 was simply that the value of a benefit for a given person depends in part on the person's level of well-being at the time that the benefit is received. Roughly, the worse off the person is the more valuable the benefit. If we accept this basic claim, it generates conclusions about applying priority to people at particular times. The claim is sufficient to support those conclusions, without the help of a theory of personal identity. It is possible that the persuasiveness of that basic claim somehow depends on our thinking about personal identity in a particular way. But the link between the moral view and personal identity is not on the surface. The view that it depends on a notion of personal identity needs to be argued for.

Initially the basic claim that the worse off a person is the more valuable the benefit is to him or her is enough to underwrite the intrapersonal application of priority. If the claim is asserted with full generality, it would make the value of benefits that I might receive at various times in my life depend in part on my level of well-being at those times. So a revisionist view of personal identity is not necessary to apply the value of priority inside a life. If we find the explanation provided by the basic claim simple and attractive, it is not easy to see what would be added by combining it with a view of different selves or the complex account of identity. We should also not be shaken by the assertion that egalitarian values require a difference in persons to be applicable. The priority view applied to people at particular times provides a good explanation of why it should not be universally true that egalitarian values can only be applied interpersonally and not intrapersonally.

The application of priority to temporal parts of lives is more convincing than the similar application of equality. So I have mostly been concerned with priority. However, I also think that applying equality to the temporal parts of different lives does not require challenging the ordinary notion of personal identity. The idea motivating the application of equality to parts of lives might simply be the thought that the inequalities between different people during temporal stages of their lives are morally important for their own sake. So an inequality favoring one person during a particular stage is not morally erased by an inequality favoring the other person during another temporal stage. This is not the same as thinking that they are in some sense different people during the different stages. However, the appeal to identity would provide the only reason for applying equality intrapersonally.

Neither the simultaneous segments view nor the corresponding segments view can be applied to a single life, so we are left with an intrapersonal application of equality that resembles the total segments view. But this application would be unreasonable if it were not based on a revisionist account of personal identity. We would not suppose that fairness requires equality between a person's youth and that same person's old age unless we accept a revisionist explanation of personal identity.

Imagine the world only contains one person. By exercising her ingenuity, she manages to live a happy life, although the quality of her life varies as she passes through the different temporal stages of life. Would it have been better if her life had a constant level of quality during each of those stages? Suppose she has deliberately chosen the inequality between the parts of her life because it will make her life as a whole better. Would we think there was a moral objection to her choice?

In chapter 4, I considered examples of deep, simultaneous inequality between stages in different lives. I thought that, in such a case, there is some intuitive support for eliminating the inequality by leveling down. Consider the same question when applied to an intrapersonal case. There is no intuitive support for reaching equality between the different temporal stages of one life by leveling down. Extending the concern for equality to temporal parts of lives is compatible with thinking that the requirement of equality applies across lives but not inside lives. There is at least some evidence that we care about inequality between the simultaneous temporal parts of different lives but no reason to think we object to inequality between the nonsimultaneous temporal parts of the same life. When equality is applied to people at particular times, it is done so interpersonally but not intrapersonally.

In chapter 4, I emphasized the problems facing the simultaneous segments view of equality. Even if there is little intuitive support for applying equality to the temporal stages in one life, the revisionist view of personal identity can provide a way of rescuing the simultaneous segments view from the objections that have been raised against it. If we accept this view of identity, it gives us a new reason for objecting to inequality between the simultaneous temporal stages of different lives. If we think of personal identity in this way, inequality between the simultaneous segments of different lives will be objectionable simply because it is tantamount to lifetime inequality between different people. Inequality between one person's current self and the current self of someone else will be important for its own sake because it cannot be compensated for at other times. The self that might be benefited at some later time will be a different self than the one that labors under the present disadvantage, so the compensation is illusory. We should not be governed by the prudential judgment about how to maximize the overall quality of a complete life since that life is lived by different selves. The prudential judgment will be objectionable since equality applies inside an ordinary life so the prudence that matters will be in terms of the best interest of particular selves, not prudence concerned with the long-term best interest of a person in the ordinary sense.

Even if we were willing to accept these radical notions, they would not support the simultaneous segments view, which only objects to inequality between the simultaneous stages in different lives. Multiple selves' analysis would object to inequality between any two selves, whether or not they exist simultaneously and whether or not they belong to what we ordinarily think of as the same life. Multiple selves analysis would support the total segments view—applied in both interpersonal and intrapersonal cases—which has little intuitive support.

6.4 FURTHER PROBLEMS FOR THE APPEAL TO PERSONAL IDENTITY

The appeal to personal identity is not necessary for applying the values of priority and equality to temporal parts of lives. Further, an appeal to personal identity is not the best way, or even a helpful way, of explaining these judgments.

In the discussion of complex views of identity, one issue is whether we psychologically identify with our putative other selves. Do we think about our so-called elderly selves as though they simply are us, or is there a failure of identification in our attitude toward them? The presence or the absence of psychological identification does not settle the philosophical issue about personal identity. Still, we strongly identify with our elderly selves. As visitors to a geriatric ward in a hospital we may be shaken by what we see. Our concern is not basically self-regarding, but we may be affected by the experience because we think that when we reach that stage of life we will be the ones subjected to indignity or patronized by the staff. Despite the deep physical, mental, and psychological changes that accompany aging, we feel that we are witnessing our own futures, and that is what frightens us. It would be less frightening if we believed that it will not be us but some other person or self only marginally related to us who will end his life in such a place.

Cases of dementia are possible exceptions to my suggestion, but even they are problematic. Children and spouses often regard the individual as still the person they loved but one who is sadly— or tragically—damaged. This thought makes their grief worse, even though it is a mistaken notion motivated by familiarity and emotion rather than a clear understanding of what it is to be a person and to be the same person. But the feeling is evidence of the strength of psychological identification, whatever we might think of its reasonableness.

Some people are disturbed at the thought that they might linger on, kept biologically alive in a hospital, after they had lost the possibility of conscious life. So they might make provisions that their lives not be allowed to end in this way. We can understand their preference, even if we might disagree with it, but I find it hard to understand someone who regards persisting in a permanent vegetative state as a catastrophe. It is easier to understand someone who is deeply frightened by the thought of ending his life as a patient in a nursing home, lost in senile dementia. The difference is partly that, in the first case, there is little or no room for psychological identification, while there is in the second.

These are reasons, although hardly decisive ones, for questioning the revisionist explanation of personal identity, at least in the case of an ordinary human life. I will now ask whether the theory about identity, assuming it was acceptable for its own sake, would give the right explanation of the moral view that applies priority and equality to parts of lives.

I believe that the badly off among the elderly would and should feel that they have a claim to our help, a claim grounded in the current state of their lives, either in their absolute condition or in how their welfare compares to the current welfare of others. According to the appeal to personal identity, a crucial part of their claim is a lack of connection between their current life and the prior stages of their lives, but the elderly do not necessarily see things that way. They might not claim that their standard of living in the past was irrelevant to the fairness of a decision to help them now, because that former prosperity was enjoyed by different people. Instead, they might contend that the present state of their lives gives rise to a reason for helping them now that is independent of what their lives were like earlier. This reason would not be made stronger if their past was miserable or weaker if their past was happy, although their past experiences might give rise to other competing reasons that bear on the question of who to help. They believe the reason grounded in the current state of their lives can at least compete with the reasons depending on complete lives that will reflect their past good or ill fortune.

Furthermore, if our concern with temporal parts of lives were explained by a weakening of personal identity, it would seem that this concern is incompatible with those dealing with lifetimes. However, our intuitive judgments seem to reveal that we feel both kinds of concern. We should apply the values of equality and priority both to people at particular times and to entire lifetimes. The account of personal identity that would support applying the values to particular times would tend to undermine their application to lifetimes.

This view of personal identity would also require changes in what we think about prudential rationality applied to one life. In Posner's view, a choice made by my young self should not determine the share of resources available to my elderly self because each version of myself should be regarded as though it were a distinct person. The view also implies that my younger self has no prudential reason to care about the welfare of the future self, although my treatment of the elderly self should be constrained by morality. Most of us find this conclusion implausible. We believe that I now have a prudential reason to care about my welfare in extreme old age, and this reason is not equivalent to a moral reason for one person to treat a different person fairly.

Parfit's less extreme view of personal identity would not have this implication, although it might support a narrowing of the temporal scope of the prudential concern and a weakening of its strength. The even less extreme view defended by McMahan would not be incompatible with also feeling moral concerns based on complete lifetimes and with preserving the importance of prudence—although, as in the case of Parfit, a weakening of psychological connections over time might mean that we should feel less concern for our future interests than the traditional notion of prudence would suppose. But Parfit's and McMahan's views become problematic when they are used to explain our apparent tendency to care about temporal stages of lives.

Neither writer fills out the view by explaining precisely what kinds of changes or how many changes are required to trigger the moral consequences he is trying to explain. The extent to which connections hold between youth and old age will differ radically in the case of different people. Since these writers do not specify a threshold of psychological change at which the implications for morality and prudence would take effect, it is possible that in almost all ordinary lives the changes are not sufficient to trigger the consequences. So it is possible that the psychological changes that occur in an ordinary life might be compatible with the traditional conception of prudence and with moral concerns that are only focused on complete lives and not on temporal parts of lives. We are not entitled to draw strong consequences from the views of Parfit and McMahan.

Another problem is that the moral judgments are not conditional on there being a significant breakdown of psychological connections in the life in question. In the example of the condominium complex and the nursing home, it is not true that the people in the nursing home should be helped only if their memory of the earlier parts of their life is clouded. They should be helped even if their recollection is perfect and their values did not change.

In chapter 5, I suggested that priority would provide a better explanation than equality of judgments that give independent importance to temporal parts of lives. It is relatively simple to apply priority to people at times. Priority can be applied intrapersonally as well as interpersonally, and its application to temporal parts of different lives and to intrapersonal cases is independent of theories of personal identity.

6.5 PRIORITY

My aim is to preserve the simplicity of the priority view. The basic claim is that a benefit is especially important if it is received by someone who is badly off. This claim is essentially about how we value well-being, not about the moral importance of the unity of a life or the moral importance of the difference between different lives. The value of a gain in well-being experienced by a given person at a given time depends in part on how well off the person is at that time—on what his current level of well-being is. When the claim is stated in that way, nothing limits the application of this idea to examples involving different people. We should also be able to say, thinking about a single person, that a benefit will be more important or valuable if it is experienced when that person is badly off. Considering the intrapersonal and the interpersonal applications, the claim does not make one application more fundamental than the other.

Of course we could choose to explicitly add a restriction to the basic claim of the priority view so that it would only apply to interpersonal cases. Thus only when we are comparing benefits received by two different people would priority be a concern. According to this view, priority is awarded to a person, to one person among others, so judgments of priority require a difference in persons. In an intrapersonal case in which a person is well off at one time but badly off at another time, there is no worse-off person to award priority to. Since she is the same person at each moment in time, there is no sense in giving priority to her when she is badly off.

One disadvantage of this approach is that it rules out explaining priority in terms of the intrinsic value of increases in well-being. If that were the appropriate explanation, priority judgments would apply inside lives. We would have to find some other way of thinking about priority that explained why priority judgments about well-being could only be made when we were comparing levels of well-being of two different people. Since the explanation in terms of well-being is both simple and appealing, this is a serious disadvantage. The simplicity of this account of priority is one of the reasons for attributing our judgments about temporal parts of lives to priority rather than equality. When the same basic claim implies that the value can be applied both interpersonally and intrapersonally, we should accept the consequence.

Jamie Mayerfeld adopts a compromise view in respect to these issues.[7] He thinks that we make priority judgments inside our lives, but he also believes that we make stronger priority judgments across lives. His priority principle is about suffering rather than well-being in general, but he understands suffering in a broad sense. He suggests that we hold both a principle based on the intrinsic value of suffering, which says the same thing in interpersonal and intrapersonal cases, and another principle of priority requiring a difference in persons that applies only to the interpersonal

---

7. Jamie Mayerfeld, *Suffering and Moral Responsibility* (New York: Oxford University Press, 1999) chapter 6.

cases. Our priority judgments are stronger in the interpersonal cases because both priority principles apply to those choices.

Mayerfeld agrees that we can apply a notion of priority inside a life. He also agrees that this application does not require appealing to personal identity. His view is more complicated than the one I have proposed. We should only hold it if we find the view intuitively compelling, where the test is whether priority for the worse off is stronger across lives than inside lives. My judgments are much the same in interpersonal and intrapersonal cases, both about well-being and about suffering more specifically. Suppose that we must choose between a small reduction in pain for S1, who is suffering intensely, and a larger reduction in suffering for S2, whose suffering is more moderate. I would at least be tempted to choose to help S1 and would reach much the same conclusion if S1 and S2 were simultaneous stages in different lives or were nonsimultaneous stages in the same life. If we feel that there is a difference in this case, it might be because the application of priority to lifetimes would be relevant to the first case but not to the second.

Suppose that I can award a benefit to someone who is currently worse off than I am. The time-specific priority view would tell me to help the other person. But suppose that if I do this it will prevent me from giving myself a benefit of the same size at some future time when I will be just as badly off as the other person currently is. If—as Mayerfeld holds—priority is stronger in a case that involves different people, then I should help the other person now and forgo the future benefit. If priority has the same strength inside and across lives because it only depends on the level of well-being of the person who receives the benefit, it does not matter which course of action I choose. In support of this view of priority, it is morally indifferent which choice I make.

6.6 PRIORITY AND PRUDENCE

My view of priority, however, faces an objection. It will be pressed by those who think that egalitarian concern must be connected to the separateness of persons. The priority principle relevant to fairness between age groups applies priority across times and across lives in exactly the same way. Just because the principle bears this feature—it applies across lives and inside lives with the same force—it does not treat a temporally extended human life as a morally important unit. How can the unity of a single life be morally important if we make exactly the same priority judgments inside one life as when we are considering two different lives? A life lived through time is a morally significant unit, and this must be acknowledged by any moral theory. This point underlies Nagel's view about compensation and the difference between interpersonal and intrapersonal judgments and is one of the arguments for restricting egalitarian judgments to the temporal scope of a complete life.

I think the objection can be answered. The time-specific priority view does not treat a temporally extended life as a morally significant unit. The view does not express that moral importance by making different judgments in interpersonal and intrapersonal cases. Yet by accepting that view, we are not denying that a temporally extended human life is a morally important unit. We should combine the view with an application of priority to lifetimes, one that treats a life as a morally important unit. The lifetime view regards human lives as units to which we should apply priority. The issue is what kind of moral importance a unified, temporally extended life has, and that will be revealed by the full range of moral judgments that we make about interpersonal and intrapersonal cases. Properly respecting the moral importance of lives does not require a deep difference in every kind of moral judgment that we make about interpersonal and intrapersonal cases. If we think that the value of a gain or loss in well-being depends on the level of well-being when a person experiences it and if we use this idea in the same way in interpersonal and intrapersonal cases, our view should not be dismissed because it conflicts with the moral importance of temporally extended human lives. We have already acknowledged that moral importance by adopting a priority principle that is concerned with lifetimes.

There is another way of defending this understanding of priority. Traditionally, egalitarians suppose that there is a fundamental distinction between interpersonal judgments and intrapersonal judgments, as in the case of Rawls and Nagel. This is because they suppose that intrapersonal judgments will turn out to be maximizing judgments, and as egalitarians they believe that interpersonal judgments should not simply maximize. But if we apply the value of priority to a single life, the judgments that will result will not simply be maximizing ones. Given priority, a person might reasonably prefer a smaller benefit when he is badly off to a larger benefit received when he is better off. If intrapersonal judgments are not maximizing, egalitarians do not have the same reason for claiming that they must be fundamentally different from interpersonal judgments. So if we apply priority in the same way inside lives and across lives, we remove the objection that egalitarians might be otherwise inclined to press.

However, there might be disagreement about how priority judgments should be characterized. Some might think that, in a case of a person making choices about his own life, the judgments are made by what is ordinarily called prudential rationality. Prudence has the goal of making a person's life as good as it can be. According to this view, prudence recognizes priority and might compel us to choose a smaller benefit when we are badly off rather than a larger benefit when we are better off. Our lives will be better if we choose the smaller benefit rather than the larger benefit. However, others might refuse to say that this choice is made by prudential rationality, thinking that prudential rationality should be understood as always choosing a larger benefit rather than a smaller benefit or always choosing less suffering rather than more suffering. The goal of prudence is simply to maximize the total amount of well-being experienced in life, irrespective of how that well-being is distributed over time. So exercising prudence would never result in choosing a smaller benefit rather than a larger benefit, even if the smaller benefit would be realized when the person was very badly off. This position implies that, if we do make priority judgments, we should see these as being distinctively moral rather than prudential.

The fact that prudence is regarded as choosing what is best for the agent in the long run is not a reason for denying that these judgments are prudential. What is best for the agent is receiving a smaller rather than a larger benefit, if the smaller benefit comes when he is badly off and if this choice makes his complete life better.[8] If we agree that the value of a benefit depends, in part, on how well off the recipient is at the time that the benefit is received, we should continue to think of the benefit as having that special value when we switch to the question of assessing the overall lifetime of the person who receives the benefit. The value of a life does not just depend on the total amount of well-being that it contains; the

---

8. This does not undermine the distinction between priority applied to lifetimes and priority applied to people at particular times. An individual's lifetime will be better overall because the benefit has special importance if it is received when he is badly off, a fact that is explained by the priority view concerned with particular times not the lifetime priority view. The lifetime priority view remains distinct because it gives priority to complete lives of low quality. It might give a benefit to someone with an unsatisfactory

value also depends on how the well-being is distributed across the temporal stages of the life. An increase in well-being when the person is badly off contributes more to the quality of the life as a whole than an increase of the same size when the person is much better off.

Someone might maintain that, even if the well-being that the person's life contained would have more value if it were distributed across time in this way, nevertheless the goal of prudential rationality is simply to maximize the total amount of well-being in the complete life and ignore the value that depends on its temporal distribution. But this way of understanding prudence seems perverse. If we are to retain our grip on the notion of value, the more valuable life should be one that it is better to live and that a person has the strongest reason to pursue. We should recognize the value of priority. Given the point of having a notion of prudential thinking in the first place, prudence should be guided by this notion of value.

The disagreement between these two views might seem to be merely verbal, but there is a way in which the issue can be understood as important. Suppose we think that a priority judgment is a distinctively moral judgment that would not be part of prudential thinking. This means that priority is not rooted in the way that we value well-being and gains in terms of well-being. A gain that

complete life who would be well off when the benefit is received rather than to someone with a better complete life who would be badly off when the benefit is received. The lifetime view can agree that assigning the benefit to the second person would do more to promote the quality of her complete life than it would in the case of the first person, but it gives priority to helping the first person because her complete life is worse. That is why I do not agree with Kappel (225) that applying priority to people at particular times means treating them as the objects of our concern rather than simply "people." On my view, if a person receives a smaller benefit at a time when he is badly off rather than a larger benefit at some other time when he is better off, it is the person, not just the person at that particular time, who is made better off.

takes someone's level of well-being from 6 to 8 does not have more value than a gain that takes someone's level of well-being from 18 to 20. The priority we give to the first gain depends on an additional moral judgment that we choose to make. It is a mistake to understand priority in this way. It would be incompatible with how Parfit and Temkin understand priority. On their view comparisons between the welfare of two different people are not required for an application of priority.

I have proposed a significant revision of prudence that would sometimes choose a smaller total amount of what was good, if the smaller total was distributed across temporal stages in a way that benefited the person when he was badly off. This interpretation of prudence also separates prudential reasoning from classical utilitarian reasoning applied to one life.

What if a person chooses to maximize the total amount of good in his life rather than respecting judgments about priority? If we accept the priority view, we think that he is making a mistake about what will make his own life best on the whole. But it does not follow that we should prevent him from carrying out his choice. He might have the right to make this decision about his own life, even if it is a mistake.

Because of the reinterpretation of prudence, my view faces another objection. The combination of applying priority inside a life and understanding prudence in the way I have suggested will seemingly undermine much of what I have said about my own account of justice between age groups. I criticize Daniels for reductionist claims that seemed questionable. His view reduces a question about interpersonal distribution to a question about intrapersonal distribution, reducing a question about distribution between life-stages to a question about lifetimes and, finally, reducing a question about justice to a question about prudence.

These criticisms will be appropriate if we think that equality should be applied interpersonally to stages of lives. But they will not be appropriate if we apply the value of priority to people at particular times, both across lives and inside lives. If we do, then the interpersonal question of distribution among the temporal stages of different lives will be equivalent to the intrapersonal question of distribution among the temporal stages of a single life, since priority will apply in the same way in each case. If we reinterpret prudence, then, in a sense, the issue about stages in lives turns out to be equivalent to an issue about lifetimes. When, in virtue of priority, we redistribute from a stage in A's life to a stage in B's life, if we imagine that the two stages had belonged to the same life, the redistribution would make that complete life better on the whole. Once prudence is reinterpreted, the application of priority could be described in terms of prudential reasoning.

One way of putting the difficulty is that if the prudential lifespan account were revised according to this view of prudence, it would escape my earlier criticisms. The priority view that I have defended could be called a variation of the prudential lifespan account. More importantly, the changes subvert the supposedly deeper explanation that I have offered for my conclusions. If the same conclusions could be reached by prudential reasoning about lifetimes, why should we think that they depend on principles that are irreducibly concerned with temporal parts of lives rather than complete lives?

I think there is a response to this criticism. Reinterpreting prudence would permit us, if we choose, to formulate the time-specific priority view as one about prudential rationality and one that is concerned with the overall quality of complete lives. But in the case of any moral theory, we can ask at what level its basic and distinctive claims are made. In the case of this view, the basic claim—that a gain has special value if it is experienced by someone who is badly off at the time the gain is received—is made about people at particular times, not about complete lives or lifetimes. It is this claim that explains and justifies the conclusions about prudence and lifetimes that the view can ultimately lead to. The view explains the conclusions it draws about peoples' well-being at particular times without beginning by considering complete lives. So the contrast between this kind of priority view and views that are fundamentally concerned with complete lives remains.

The view I have defended does not represent the strongest possible way of caring independently about temporal parts of lives. The view contends that it can be reasonable for a person to increase his well-being at a particular time even at a cost of decreasing the total amount of well-being in his life as a whole. But the view does not claim that it can be reasonable to make your life better during a particular temporal stage at the cost of making your complete life worse, because when a person applies priority inside his life, he is making his life as a whole better. His complete life may contain a smaller total amount of well-being, but because of priority, it counts as a better life.

We can imagine views that would reach stronger conclusions. They might allow, for example, that it might be reasonable for me to make my middle age better at the cost of making my complete life worse. Some might think that this much more radical departure from the traditional conception of prudence is defensible. They might appeal to persuasive criticisms of the traditional view of prudence, for example, Parfit's sympathetic description of the rejection of temporal neutrality.

However, I am not convinced that the stronger views would be defensible in any form that is relevant to the issues I am discussing. It would be irrational to give myself the best possible adolescence if the result will be making my life as a whole worse.

Even if I am too pessimistic about the prospects of the stronger views, I do not want to make my explanation of justice to the elderly depend on their being defensible. The conclusions about justice between age groups that I have tried to defend are intuitively persuasive, and that is a reason to look for a less contested view to explain them.[9]

We can apply this view of priority to the example in chapter 1. The people in the nursing home are much worse off in terms of resources, subjective well-being, and in terms of most plausible objective accounts of the quality of lives. The elderly people are living such miserable lives the resources will actually benefit them more than the younger people. Yet this explanation will often not be available. Age, infirmity, and illness have damaged the people in the nursing home and weakened their ability to use resources to improve their lives. This is especially likely to be the case if their cognitive abilities have been severely damaged. So we are really asking the better-off people to accept a larger sacrifice for the sake of a smaller gain for their neighbors. The explanation might come from a principle about equality or priority. The transfer would reduce inequality even though the benefits it generates are smaller than the harm it imposes on the young, and it would also help the people who are worse off and have lives of very low quality in an absolute sense.

9. There is another advantage to reinterpreting prudence so that it acknowledges the priority of receiving a benefit at a time when the recipient is badly off. In chapter 4, I pointed out that the simultaneous segments view about equality conflicts with prudence. It recommends distributing resources between the simultaneous temporal stages of different lives with a view to reducing inequality between those stages. It concedes that one consequence might be that resources are distributed inside lives in a way that prudential rationality would reject. However, according to the view about priority I have suggested, there will be no conflict. Prudential rationality and moral thinking that considers what people who are young might owe to those who are old will reach the same conclusions. In this way the view escapes the objection based on prudence explained in chapter 2.

But in order to defend the transfer, both values must be applied to temporal stages in lives. The transfer reduces present inequality, but it does not necessarily reduce inequality between lifetimes—it might even increase it. The transfer involves a loss for people who are better off and a gain for people who are worse off, but it does not help the people whose lives assessed as temporal wholes are the worst.

The priority view provides a stronger foundation than equality for such a transfer. The special moral concern that I believe we have with temporal stages in lives does not require support from a revisionist view of personal identity. The concern depends on a special kind of moral value—not a special way of understanding personal identity—that applies in much the same way across lives and inside lives. A benefit has a special importance if it is received by someone who is badly off. Prudential thinking does not acknowledge this special importance, since it aims at maximizing the total amount of what is good. We should revise our understanding of prudence to take this special importance into account; doing so would not collapse my account of fairness between age groups into the prudential lifespan account or endorse the view that all moral concerns are ultimately based on lifetimes, rather than on temporal parts of lives. The new understanding of prudence would itself be explained by the more fundamental idea of priority—the claim that a benefit has a special importance or value when it is received by someone who is badly off. We would revise our notion of what makes a complete life go best by moral considerations that we discover when we think about a person at a particular time during the course of the life.

Chapter 7

Changes in Values over Time

7.1 PRUDENCE AND CHANGING GOALS

Prudence does not provide a correct principle of just distribution between age groups. However, it is obvious that when we consider our own lives and the lives of other people, we often must think about those lives as temporal wholes extended through time. This is the traditional task of prudential thinking, which we need to apply in planning our own futures. We also must think in this way when considering principles of distribution for lifetimes. One important aim of the institution of social security is to make lifetimes as good as they can be—although, again, I have argued that this aim does not by itself decide whether the institution is operating fairly.

When we think in this way we are not just considering how to distribute well-being across the different temporal parts of our lives. There are many other difficult questions that need to be answered in order for prudence to achieve its goal.

One problem concerns a person's preferences or goals and values. Almost everyone agrees that these goals and values, and the extent to which they are achieved, are important factors for a person's well-being, although there is disagreement about how their influence on well-being can best be understood. When we are thinking about a complete life, the problem is that goals and values will change during that life, and it may well be that what the person values during some temporal stage of her life she strongly rejects during some other stage. How should we accommodate these changes when deciding what would make the person's life best as a whole?

The problem is not just theoretical. When we think about our own lives—and particularly about ourselves in extreme old age—we are alive to the likelihood of such a change in our values. We may believe that our concerns at that time in our life will have altered for the worse, and this might affect the provision that we are now willing to make for that part of our life. This feeling will be especially strong if we anticipate a decline into dementia. We may see no value at all in the life we would be living in that eventuality and think that the existence of such a stage in our lives will reduce the value and meaning of those lives as wholes.

The treatment the problem receives in this chapter does not depend on my view that prudential thinking should incorporate the value of priority. The points I make apply to both the traditional view that prudence aims at maximizing the total amount of well-being in a life and the alternative view of prudence I proposed.

Typically our goals and values change in the course of our lives.

These changes can create conflicts. Suppose that my present goals and the goals that I will endorse when I am old are significantly different. Choices that I could make now might help me to realize my present goals but hinder my ability to eventually realize my future goals because the resources available for me to use over my lifetime are limited. However, in speaking of conflict, I will assume not just that there is competition for scarce resources but that there is a direct disagreement about value between myself now and myself at the later time. I now believe that goal G1 is more important than goal G2, but at that future time I will instead think that G2 is more important than G1. Although I will consider other examples, the basic case I will discuss is a conflict between what my current goals would mandate if they were applied to my life at the future time T2 and what the goals I will hold at T2 would recommend about my life at T2. I call this a present-future conflict.

The conflict raises an issue about how we should think when we make a decision that will affect our future. How should prudential thinking respond to the change in values? Should I simply use my current goals for a decision that is to be made now or just my future goals when it is a matter of evaluating the facts that will obtain at that future time? Or is it more reasonable to somehow take both sets of goals into account?

My discussion will be governed by an assumption that I call modest objectivism. I assume that some goals can be more important or more valuable in themselves than others and that people can make mistakes when they make judgments about the importance of specific goals. I think this assumption is reasonable, but I will not argue for it here. However, it does distinguishes my view from those that refuse to question or challenge the preferences that people have at particular times.

I call the assumption "modest" objectivism because I do not suppose that appealing to the objective value of goals is enough to solve the problem. That is, we should not conclude that the reasonable choice in the present-future case is to further the goal that has the greatest objective value, irrespective of whether it is a goal that the person now accepts or a goal that she will eventually accept in the future.

There are three main responses to the problem of conflicting goals. These views share a certain assumption about the nature of the problem. They suppose that the basic issue is about time and the intrinsic importance of time for rational decision making. Consequently, these views suppose that a solution will identify some attitude toward the significance of time as being reasonable. Once this basic attitude has been identified, it will tell us whether we should take into account all of our goals, only our present goals, or only our predicted future goals when it is a matter of evaluating facts or events at that future time.

None of the three solutions is convincing. They face intuitive and more theoretical objections, which should motivate a different approach to the problem. Instead of attempting to identify some attitude toward time as uniquely rational, we should regard the problem as being partly a matter of understanding the nature of well-being.

A particular view about well-being—a view that I call the positive response condition—provides the best explanation of our judgments about which choices are reasonable in cases of changing goals. If we accept this condition, a particular choice will be reasonable, not because it correctly responds to the rational significance of time itself but because it is the choice that will maximize the agent's well-being.

7.2 THE PRUDENTIAL SOLUTION

The first view might seem to be the solution offered by traditional theories of prudence, although not all defenders of the rationality of prudence see it as having this implication about changes in values. Because of this connection, I call it the prudential solution. The basic claim is that decision making, in order to be rational, should be governed by a strong requirement of temporal neutrality. Mere differences in timing, or facts about when things occur, cannot in themselves affect our reasons for acting, so we should ignore those facts when making a decision.

This idea is thought to lead to the conclusion that we should take all of our goals equally into account when making a decision that will affect our lifetime, irrespective of the particular times at which we might endorse those goals during our lives. In my example, it would be a mistake for the person at T1 to take into account only her goals at T1 about the later time T2, but it would be equally a mistake for her to decide at T1 merely on the basis of the goals that she believes she will possess at T2. Both those decisions would involve an objectionable bias in favor of some particular time. Temporal neutrality requires that she should be impartial about both her current goals for her life at T2 and the goals that she will have when T2 arrives. She needs to strike some kind of balance between the conflicting goals.

One problem for this solution is that it clashes with modest objectivism. If some goals can be deemed more important than others, it is difficult to understand how there could be a rational requirement for an agent to give equal weight to all of the different goals that she might espouse during her lifetime. After all, her goals at T2 might actually be much more valuable than the goals that she held for T2 earlier in her life at T1, even though she did not recognize this fact at T1. In that case, it would not be reasonable for her to give her goals at T1 the same weight as her goals at T2.

Of course this objection will not impress someone who rejects objectivism. A claim could also be made that this strong form of temporal neutrality would only be endorsed by someone who did not believe that goals could differ in objective value. Since I find modest objectivism persuasive, I do not see this as a satisfying reply to the objection.

A more complicated reply to the objection would distinguish between what is objectively reasonable and what is subjectively reasonable. Modest objectivism about goals might be part of an answer to the first question. If goal G1 is objectively more valuable than goal G2, that is a reason for thinking that it is objectively more rational to choose to realize G1 than to choose to realize G2. But we can also talk about what it would be subjectively rational for an agent to choose. Subjective rationality depends on the agent's beliefs about what reasons she has for acting, whether those beliefs are true or false.

However, the prudential solution does not seem to be intended merely as a theory about what is subjectively rational. If it were, it would not be a plausible theory. If subjective rationality is understood in terms of a person's beliefs about what it is rational to do, those beliefs might mandate that she should use her goals at T1 to make decisions about T2, rather than giving equal weight to both sets of goals. If she believes at T1 that it is rational to decide using the goals she holds at T1, how can it be subjectively rational for her to give equal weight to both sets of goals?[1]

However, modest objectivism is not the main reason why people have felt dissatisfaction with the prudential solution. Nagel—who passionately defends the rationality of prudence in general—is not completely satisfied with the prudential solution.[2] He comments that one might respond to changes in goals in this way, but that

---

1. It might be denied that what it is subjectively rational for an agent to do at a particular time must be explained in terms of the beliefs about the reasons for acting that the agent holds at that particular time. Perhaps it can also depend on goals and beliefs about reasons for acting that she holds at other times. In that case, subjective rationality might require her to give weight to her future goals as well as her present goals, even if she does not now believe that this is what it is rational for her to do. I will not argue against this suggestion, but I think it will be difficult to make a convincing case that the prudential solution is the best account of subjective rationality.
2. Nagel, *Possibility*, 74n1.

one also might respond by relying on one's present goals and values to make decisions about the future. He points out that, if prudence adopts the solution I have described, it would treat goals and values as if they were merely preferences by assigning them equal weight. Nagel apparently does not see this point as a criticism of the solution, but Parfit regards it as a damaging criticism.[3] Since accepting something as a goal involves a commitment to its value or importance, it might be unreasonable to find a compromise by assigning equal weight to values that one endorses and values that one currently rejects.

The prudential solution's conclusion about present-future examples is also implausible. In Nagel's example, a person who now values spontaneity, risk, and strong emotion knows that 20 years in the future he will value security and tranquillity. Suppose that he is considering a choice that he can make now that would compel him to embark on a dangerous adventure 20 years from now. In making his decision, it can seem odd that he should be rationally required to give equal weight to his current values, given that he will have abandoned those values when that future time arrives.

Parfit thinks it is clear that the individual should now give no weight at all to the view he held about his future when he was an adolescent, the view that he should spend his life as a poet. This is a case of past-present conflict. Some people will find the example so compelling that they would make it a condition of the solution to the problem of changing goals that it should agree with Parfits's conclusion about goals that we used to endorse but no longer value. Because the prudential solution endorses neutrality among goals, the prudential solution also fails this test.

3. Parfit, *Reasons,* 154–55.

Finally, it is not clear that the prudential solution is supported by temporal neutrality. That idea means, roughly, having an equal concern for every temporal stage in one's life. But the person who uses her current goals to make decisions about a later time when her goals will be different is not necessarily violating that requirement. It is not that she does not care about her distant future or that she cares less about it than she cares about the present. She cares about her future a great deal, which is why she thinks it is important to use the right set of goals in making decisions that will profoundly affect her life at that time. Her mistake, if we think that it is a mistake, is in letting her present goals represent her concern about a future time when she will be committed to different goals. That mistake does not obviously involve a pure time preference that violates temporal neutrality.

It might be claimed that it is a violation of temporal neutrality at a higher level. She chooses to follow her present goals rather than her future goals, which is just a more complicated form of a bias in favor of present goals. But it is questionable whether this is the right assessment. We could instead say that she acts on those goals because they are the ones she accepts and is committed to, the ones that she thinks are genuinely valuable. Of course the goals that she accepts and is committed to now must be her present goals, but that does not necessarily mean that she acts on them because they are her present goals. Her attitude does not need to be construed as believing these goals are the appropriate ones for her to realize simply because they are her present goals, and believing also that a person's present goals as such always outweigh goals they may hold at other times. So it is not clear that her stance depends on giving greater importance to the present than to other times.

Given the problems for the prudential solution, there is a more appealing way of understanding temporal neutrality. In present-future cases, the agent is not required to give equal weight to his present and future values. He is only required not to give them unequal weight in virtue of some fact about timing. In other words, he should not give more weight to his present values because they are his present values. But temporal neutrality does not, for example, forbid him from giving more weight to his present values on the grounds that they are in themselves more important or more reasonable than his future values.

We could revise prudence using this understanding of temporal neutrality. Then there would be no conflict with modest objectivism. My positive view will be compatible with this notion of temporal neutrality, but I will argue later that this understanding of prudence needs to be supplemented by other ideas to properly handle cases of changing goals.

7.3 THE PRESENT-AIM VIEW

The second solution to the problem of conflicting values holds that a person should act on her present values in making decisions that will affect her life at later times when her values will be different. This answer is radically different from the first. It seems to give an importance to time that the first solution would reject on principle and is undeniably focused on the present in that it claims that, when we make a decision, we should use the values that we hold at the time the decision is made.

This solution is defended by Parfit. He develops the view in opposition to the prudential solution, and he argues that it escapes the objections to the prudential solution. Parfit considers it as falling under a more general theory of reasons for acting that he calls the "present-aim theory." I will use this name, although I am interested in it specifically as a response to changes in values and not as a general account of reasons for action.

There are two interesting features about Parfit's discussion. First, he treats the present-aim view as a theory of subjective rationality. Nagel did not draw a distinction between subjective and objective rationality. Second, Parfit narrows the range of cases that he is considering. He says that the points he wants to make are clearer if we consider desires or goals that rest on moral beliefs and comments that Nagel's examples concern ideals about how we should live our own lives rather than explicit moral principles. For Parfit, a suitable example might be someone whose beliefs about justice change between youth and old age.

Parfit thinks it is clear that the present-aim view is more accurate than the prudential solution. He comments that the prudential solution asks an agent to give the same weight to values that she currently accepts and to values that she currently rejects, and argues that this is obviously an unreasonable demand to impose. Presumably his confidence is explained by his decision to talk about what is subjectively rational. It is plausible to think that it is subjectively rational to act on the values we currently accept.

The present-aim view does not allow merely future goals (goals that we will only come to accept in the future) to have any bearing on present decisions in present-future examples. It also does not allow merely past goals (goals that we accepted in the past but later abandoned) to influence present decisions in past-present examples. Parfit emphasizes the latter point in contrasting the present-aim view with the prudential solution. This aspect of the view is persuasive, but it also points to a feature of the theory that is less intuitively acceptable. In present-future examples, the present-aim view permits our present goals to influence our future lives at times when we will no longer endorse those goals. It tells the man in Nagel's example to act on his present desire to face dangers in the distant future, despite his knowledge that at that future time he will value safety and security. The present-aim view is more radical than the prudential solution, since it holds that he should only consult his present goals while the prudential solution asks him to take into account both his present and future goals. If he acts on the present-aim theory, the result will be that his life in the future will be determined by goals that are merely former goals at that stage in his life. So in that way, the present-aim view permits merely past goals to influence a present choice, although the supposed unreasonableness of this was offered as a reason for preferring the present-aim theory to classical prudence.

Like the prudential solution, the present-aim theory conflicts with modest objectivism. My goals at T1 about T2 might have some value, but they might have much less value than my goals at T2 about T2. So it would not be reasonable to give the first set of goals dominant weight and the second set of goals no weight.

Given Parfit's account of the present-aim view, the obvious reply will be that the view is only intended to be a theory of subjective rationality. That was unconvincing as a defence of the prudential solution, but the present-aim view is much more persuasive as a theory of subjective rationality. If we understand "X is subjectively rational for A" as "A believes that X is rational" and apply this view to a person at a particular time, then the present-aim view seems to be the obviously correct account of what it is subjectively rational for a person to choose at a time, including the agents in examples of changing goals.

However, being interpreted as an account of subjective rationality is not an unmixed advantage for the present-aim view. If the view is understood in this way, its status as the correct theory of subjective rationality is a simple consequence of the definition of subjective rationality. This is not the source for the present-aim view that its proponents seem to envisage. It is no longer based on a view about the significance of time for rational choice that assigns a special importance to the present as opposed to the past and the future. The present is singled out because the issue of how we should reasonably respond to a change in values has been reduced to the question, "What would it be subjectively rational for the agent to choose at time T1?" We do not learn anything important about either rationality or time when we see that the answer to that question depends on the goals that the agent believes to be valuable at T1.

Moreover, many of us think that rationality can be objective as well as subjective. We might suspect that the most important issue will be what it is objectively rational to do in cases of changing values. If we defend the present-aim view in the way that I have described, then there is no reason to think it will have any role to play in the account of objective rationality.

Faced with these problems, someone might try to connect the present-aim view with objective rationality. However, the present-aim position cannot be all there is to objective rationality—if my present goal is objectively worthless and my future goal has great objective value it cannot be rational to act simply on the basis of my present goal. Perhaps, however, the special importance of the present can be regarded as at least one factor in determining objective rationality. The fact that I am now committed to a certain goal might contribute to the objective rationality of my decision to pursue that goal, even if it can be outweighed by other factors that are also relevant to determining what is objectively rational. I am not sure whether this possibility is worth exploring, but the view that would result would bear little resemblance to the present-aim view and would have to be explained and defended in a different way.

We cannot support this view just by pointing out that an agent will at least believe that the action that furthers his current goals is rational.

7.4 THE SIMULTANEOUS VALUES VIEW

The third answer to the problem of changing goals resembles the second in one respect. It identifies a particular time such that it is the goals that one holds at that time that should determine decisions in cases of changing goals. However, it does not single out the time at which the decision is made for this special status. Instead, it picks out the time at which the relevant consequences of the decision will occur. It does not appeal to the goals the agent holds at T1 concerning T2 in the way that the second solution does (assuming that T1 is the present and the time at which the decision is made). Instead it appeals to the goals that the agent will hold later at T2 when the effects of the earlier decision will be realized.

About merely past goals the third solution agrees with the present-aim view that they should not influence a decision made at T1 about T1. However, the solution disagrees with the present-aim view about present-future cases. The second solution claims that merely future goals—goals concerning T2 that you will hold at T2 but do not hold at the earlier time T1—should not influence a decision made at T1 about T2. The third solution takes the opposite view, stating that it is the goals that you will hold at T2 that should determine a decision made at T1 about your life at T2.

The present-aim view is naturally expressed in terms of tense, the distinction between past, present, and future. It holds that when a person makes a decision, the values it is reasonable to apply are those she accepts when the decision is made, and those values are her present ones. Merely past values and merely future values are excluded. The third solution is most naturally expressed in a way that does not mention past, present, and future. In assessing a change in a person's life that occurs at T1, the values to be applied are the values that the person holds at T1. When we make decisions about T1, this principle will sometimes ask us to appeal to present values, sometimes to future values, and sometimes to past values (for example, when we are judging the significance of some event in our life in the past), depending on the relationship between T1 and the time at which our decision is made. I will call the third solution the simultaneous values view, because it maintains that the relevant values are those that the agent accepts simultaneously with the temporal part of his life that is being evaluated.

Krister Bykvist defends a particular version of the third response,[4] arguing that its conclusion about Nagel's example—the man should not compel himself to face dangers at some future time when he will be deeply averse to taking risks—is much more persuasive than that of the second solution. However, Bykvist's version of the view does not completely ignore our past preferences. He thinks that a preference at T1 to be a poet at T2 has no weight if, at T2, one will prefer to be a philosopher. However, if the past preference is supported by one's current preference (that is, if the past preference and the present preference correspond) then the past preference matters for its own sake. So if at T2, I still wish to be a poet, my reasons for being a poet at T2 are stronger because I held this preference in the past as well as the present. Suppose that at T2 I come to have a brand-new preference to be an athlete, which is equal in strength to my preference at T2 to be

4. Krister Bykvist, "The Moral Relevance of Past Preferences" in *Time and Ethics: Essays at the Intersection*, H. Dyke, ed., (Dordrecht Kluwer Academic Publishers, 2003,115–36).

a poet. According to Bykvist, I have stronger reasons at T2 to be a poet than to be an athlete, because the first present preference has the additional support of my past preference while the second present preference does not.

Like the other solutions, Bykvist's proposal conflicts with modest objectivism. The goals concerning T2 that I hold at T2 may be less valuable than the goals concerning T2 that I held at T1, so a modest objectivist would not necessarily agree that my decisions about T2 should be based on the values I hold at T2. However, Bykvist sets objectivism aside. He assumes that my preferences at T1 and T2 cannot be criticized or rationally assessed, so that we cannot say that my goals at T1 are either more or less reasonable or valuable than my goals at T2.

Nevertheless, his solution to the problem of changing goals is a version of objective rationality, not subjective rationality. He thinks that, in this example, it is rational for me to make my choice at T1 on the basis of the goals I will hold at T2, not the goals that I hold at T1. If, instead, I were to make the choice in accordance with my goals at T1 because I thought that was the reasonable thing to do, Bykvist would say that I was making a mistake.

Bykvist provides a rationale for the view. He says that a person is a self-identical entity that persists through time, but at any given time it is a temporal stage of that person that has preferences. On his view, a person can be seen as a related series of person stages. Bykvist believes that a view of reasons for action should reflect both of these aspects of a person. A person stage should have a say in what happens to it, but it is questionable that it should get a say in what happens to other person stages. Allowing a person's past values to determine his present reasons for action would violate the autonomy of the person stage that holds a set of values now, in the present. However, a view that claims that only a person's present reasons and goals matter for his present actions—as the present-aim theory contends—is mistaken because it ignores the significance of the fact of the continuing self-identical person and that we live our lives partly from a diachronic perspective. So Bykvist presents his view as properly respecting both aspects of our lives in time. Because of the importance of a particular person stage, present goals and values outweigh past or future goals and values when there is a conflict (again assuming the agent is assessing his life in the present). But past values should be credited with some importance in their own right when they match the person's present values.

Bykvist, in what he says about the importance of a person stage, is adopting a view about personal identity that many will reject. Even if we do not object to his rationale in this way, it is not clear that it justifies the conclusions that he draws. Suppose we grant that both the continuing person and the person stage are significant and that a view about reasons for action should reflect the importance of both. We might think this gives us a reason to count present values as being more important than the values we hold at other times, but Bykist gives them lexical priority. Values held at other times in life only matter at all if they agree with one's present values. If we think that both the continuing person and the person stage matter, why should we draw such a one-sided conclusion?

I have criticized Bykvist's rationale. Nevertheless, the view seems more reasonable than either the prudential solution or the present-aim view. It matches the judgments we would make about present-future and past-present cases. In Nagel's example, the application of the view tells the man not to commit himself to dangerous adventures in the future. The prudential solution and the present-aim view have problems accounting for those judgments.

7.5 THE ROLE OF WELL-BEING

The positive view that I will defend resembles Bykvist's in that it reaches many of the same conclusions about the examples. However, it gives a different explanation of those conclusions.

Unlike the views considered so far, this one is designed to be compatible with modest objectivism about goals and values. It also differs from them in another way. The three views I have already considered define the problem of changing goals as one about the relationship between time and rationality. To answer the problem, they look for some attitude toward time that counts as rationally required. The prudential solution thinks that rationality requires temporal neutrality. We should see the different times in our lives as having equal importance, and on this basis, we should conclude that the reasonable thing to do is to take both sets of goals into account. The present-aim view believes in the fundamental importance of the temporal divisions of past, present, and future. It holds that, because of that importance, a reasonable agent who makes a decision should use the goals that he endorses at that time, not goals that he held or will hold at other times but which now belong to the past or future. The simultaneous values view focuses not on the time at which the decision is made but on the time at which that decision will impact the agent's life. It proposes that the agent should decide using the goals he will have when his life is changed, not the goals he may endorse at the time of the decision that leads to the change. The last two views give a special importance to the present, though not in the same way, or rather they identify a different present as being especially relevant to the decision.

The final view does not look for a response to the problem in some general attitude toward the significance of time. Instead, it appeals to how we should understand welfare or well-being. In examples of the sort I have considered, the agent will typically decide by thinking about which action will best promote her own welfare. She wants to make the decision that will make her life better on the whole.

My account of well-being also involves objectivism. Just as I have assumed that some goals can be more important than others, I also presume that achieving a more important goal will better promote a person's well-being than achieving a less important goal. However, I do not think well-being is simply determined by the objective value of states or activities. There is another relevant factor. The agent should also positively respond to the valuable state or activity if well-being is to be maximized. There will be different views about the nature of this response. Some might see it as positively evaluating the activity, others as welcoming it or enjoying it, as desiring the activity, or as some combination of these responses. The response condition might also be given different degrees of strength. Some might contend that anything that receives the positive response contributes to the agent's well-being to some extent irrespective of its objective value. Others might think that activities that do possess objective value will not contribute to well-being at all unless the agent positively responds to them in the appropriate way.

For my purposes, it is not necessary to answer these questions. The important thing is that positive response is a factor in determining well-being just as objective value is. In the following, I will use a relatively weak account of its strength and will assume that it influences well-being at least to the extent that a person might receive more well-being from a less valuable activity that they positively respond to than from a more valuable activity that they do not positively respond to.

The positive response condition applies to cases in which values change. If at T1 I hold values that are strikingly different from the values that I will hold at T2 and if I use my values at T1 to make a decision at T1 that will affect T2, then at T2 I will not positively respond to the change I have brought about. That would reduce the amount of well-being that I will experience at T2. Reaching this conclusion does not depend on supposing that my values at T2 are more reasonable than my values at T1. Whether I think about this question before or after the change in my values, I will reach the same conclusion about the effect of the decision on whether the positive response condition will be satisfied at T2.[5]

Suppose Alice is a writer thinking about her old age when her active career will be over. She now believes that the best thing she can do in old age would be to preserve her legacy as a writer. She might advise younger writers, prepare revised editions of her books, and lecture at university campuses, but she also knows that when she is old her mind will have changed. She will then most want to engage in the kind of social activities that she neglected when she was younger, and she will also come to think that this is the most worthwhile way to spend her final years. Suppose that there is some course of action she could take that would lock herself into the first kind of life in her old age. What choice should she make?

Suppose that her earlier view about value is the correct one. Social activities in retirement would have some value but not as much as a continued devotion to literature. Nevertheless, this

---

5. The same cannot be said about the objective value determinant of well-being. My judgment of the objective value of what happens at T2 will be different depending on whether I make this judgment at T1 or T2, so my view about the amount of well-being that I will experience at T2 will also differ depending on whether I am relying on my values at T1 or my values at T2.

consideration does not settle the question of what choice she should make, given that she is concerned with maximizing her own well-being. Literary activities would have more value than social ones, but if she chooses them the positive response condition will not be satisfied when she engages in them. If she makes a choice now that allows her to engage in social activities during retirement, it will be satisfied. So it is possible that she will have a higher level of welfare in old age if her life is centered on the social activities, and she can appreciate this when she makes her decision.

The example shows how this view is compatible with modest objectivism. We can reach the conclusion that most people would think correct, even though we admit that the literary activities would have more objective value than the social ones. Since the positive response condition is only one determinant of well-being, in another case the better choice might be to lock oneself in to activities that one would not appreciate at the time one in engaged in them. The example also shows that the view about well-being can explain judgments that might seem to favor one of the other theories previously discussed. In this case, the view reaches the same conclusion as Bykvist's, but the conclusion does not depend on the blanket claim made by the simultaneous values view that the decision about her old age should be made simply on the strength of the values that she will hold when she is old. Her views in old age about the respective values of literary and social activities are mistaken. If she thinks in terms of well-being, she can decide against locking herself into a literary life even if she uses her present values in making the decision. There is a sense in which her values during old age do determine the decision that she should make earlier in her life but not because they have a unique importance for her decision simply because they are the values that she will endorse when she is old. These values matter because they determine whether the positive response condition on well-being will be met during her old age. Since my view accepts objectivism about goals while Bykvist's does not, the two views arrive at different conclusions in other examples.

By discussing changes in goals in terms of well-being, I am not assuming the egoistic view that choosing rationally requires maximizing one's own long-term well-being. That theory of rationality is mistaken. However, one's own well-being is one goal among others that it is rational to pursue, although it might well be outweighed by other goals. In Nagel's example and in my examples, the agent's concern is with living her life in the way that is best in terms of well-being.

I mentioned that Parfit moves away from examples about ideals applied to one's own life and considers examples about the moral treatment of other people. We can now understand the significance of this. In Nagel's examples, the change in ideals can influence the positive response condition and so affect the agent's future well-being. But in the case of a moral commitment to a principle of justice, the fact that I will later endorse a false principle of justice does not mean that the unjust actions I perform in following that mistaken principle will be less unjust because I accept that principle when I perform them. So Parfit was right to think that, in the moral examples, there is less reason for the agent to give weight to his future change of mind.

This view does not produce a solution to the problem by retreating to a description of subjective rationality. The ideas in the view are part of a theory of objective rationality, although of course they do not amount to a complete theory of objective rationality. In my example, it is objectively unreasonable for the writer to lock herself into a life of literary activity in her old age. If she reached the conclusion that it was a rational thing to do, she would be making a mistake.

The example of the writer suggests a qualification of the view. Perhaps some nonmoral ideals should be treated in the way Parfit treats moral ideals. The writer might attach great value to literature and to activities associated with it, and let us again suppose that she is objectively right to do so. She might think that it is more important to maintain her commitment to a literary life for the sake of literature rather than for her own sake. She does not believe that this choice would best promote her own well-being; she believes she should live in this way because of the value of literature even though it diminishes her well-being. I would not argue that someone would be unreasonable to think in this way. It might make sense to sacrifice your own well-being for the sake of literature just as it makes sense to sacrifice your well-being for the sake of justice. But this is not the example that I have been discussing. In my example, the agent is concerned with her own well-being, but she is not sure what to do given that her goals will change over time.

However, this variation on the original example can help us choose between the view I have defended and the simultaneous values view. Suppose that the writer is concerned with aesthetic value, not with her own well-being. Still, she must face the problem that her current judgment of the aesthetic value of the literary activities possible in her old age differs radically from the judgment she will make when she is old. She now thinks that particular kind of postscript to her writing career would have considerable aesthetic value, but when she is old she will believe instead that such quasiliterary activities are merely pretentious. Bykvist's would contend that she should use the goals that she will hold in the future to make a choice that will affect her life at that future time. She should make her decision now in accordance with the aesthetic judgment she will make when she is old, even though we are now supposing that the reduction in her future well-being that would result if she used her present judgment instead is not a relevant consideration. But this conclusion has little plausibility, once the question of aesthetic value has been separated from its effects on the agent's well-being. Why should we think it is irrational for her to choose on the basis of her current beliefs about aesthetic value? This suggests that, when we find Bykvist's conclusions persuasive, it is because we are being influenced by considerations about well-being.

However, there is a problem for this answer to the problem of changing goals. It might be true that at T2 I will have less well-being if my life fits my past values at T1 rather than the new values that I will hold at T2. Suppose that, for this reason, I decide at T1 that my life at T2 should match my values at T2. Making this choice will presumably reduce my well-being at T1 (and at all subsequent times until the change in my values occurs) when I look forward to my life at T2. Why should we think that considering well-being will lead to the conclusion about the example that intuitively seems the right one, that I should be guided by the values that I will hold at T2?

This might seem a fundamental objection. In applying the positive response condition, I have looked for a positive response by the agent at the time he performs the activity. This restriction can seem unmotivated. If the agent positively responds to the activity at some other time—before or after the activity is performed— why could this not contribute to his well-being?

In considering this objection we should distinguish between two different ways in which the positive response condition can contribute to well-being. The first concerns the hedonic aspect of well-being. If at T1 I do not positively respond to my life at

T1 then, this will cause me distress at T1 and lower my level of well-being at that point. This effect can also occur across time. If in a present-future case I choose to act on my future values, this will cause me distress in the present when I look to the future. If I make a decision about my present life on the strength of my present values rather than my future values, I will feel distress in the future when I retrospectively look back at my choice.

This assessment is not a strong objection to my view. We should take the pleasure and distress felt at other times into account, but it is typically the case that the distress I feel in the present if my present life clashes with my present values will be greater than the prospective or retrospective distress in these examples. The view is still able to support the conclusions about the examples that seem reasonable.

However, there is another way the agent's positive response might influence well-being. If I perform valuable activities, the fact that I also positively respond to or approve of those activities might enhance the value of the activities and contribute in that way to my well-being. The extra value is not a matter of my feeling pleasure for what I have done. The activities will have more value in virtue of my positive response than if I had performed them without positively responding to them and without believing that they were valuable and worthwhile. I call this the value enhancement reading of the positive response condition.

This is a more challenging and more controversial claim to make about positive response and value. Some writers about well-being will reject it, but others will accept it. I will not try to defend the claim but will use it to answer the objection that it was arbitrary to restrict the positive response condition to a positive response in the present to an activity performed in the present. I may not positively respond to a valuable activity when I engage in it, but if, at a later time, I retrospectively endorse and appreciate its value, some might hold that this can also influence the value of the activity and the quality of my life.

One difference between the value enhancement version and the hedonic version of the positive response condition is that, in the case of hedonic goods, the increase of my well-being would be temporally located at the later time from which I look back at the activity and enjoy it. But if we believe in retrospective value enhancement, it seems more natural to temporally locate the increase in well-being at the earlier time at which the valuable activity was performed, not at the later time at which I positively respond to what I did in the past. My retrospective approval at T2 enhances the quality of my life at T1, in the sense that it makes my life at T1 better than it would have been if I had never at any time in my life appreciated the value of the activity that I performed at T1.

Retrospective value enhancement seems easier to accept than prospective value enhancement. In present-future cases, we would not say that my present prospective approval of a future life that matches my present values but will clash with my future values provides a reason based on well-being to lock myself into such a future. We would simply think that, when the future arrives, the positive response condition will not be satisfied, and we will draw the appropriate conclusion about my future well-being. Prospective value enhancement is not a threat to my view.

However, retrospective approval has more significance. If at the end of my life I am fortunate enough to see the value in things I accomplished in the past when previously I did not take them seriously, this might redeem the value of my past. Suppose an artist created excellent paintings during his career but did not value what he was doing. But in his later years, he begins to value his paintings and his own talent for what they were worth. This belated recognition does not make the pictures themselves better or worse, but it might influence our judgment about his well-being and how good a life he has lived. He is not permanently alienated from his own most important accomplishments.

Nevertheless, even in this example, retrospective approval does not give his activities as much value as they would have had if he had positively responded to them while he was engaged in them. As long as appreciation of the activity when it is performed has a greater effect on value than retrospective appreciation, then my point stands. Well-being provides a reason for using the values I will hold at T1 when I make a decision that will affect my life at T1, and so it supports an answer to the problem of changing goals.

Proposing an asymmetry between prospective and retrospective approval might also threaten my account. I have said that the basic claim is about well-being, not the significance of time. However, perhaps prospective approval does not enhance value because the relevant values belong to the past when the valuable activity is performed. Retrospective approval is more effectual because, although the person does not already endorse his future values when the activity is performed, at least those values have not already been rejected and consigned to the past. These are points about time. Accepting the asymmetry gives some importance to facts about time. Nevertheless, if the asymmetry holds, retrospective approval contributes to well-being in a way that prospective approval does not, and this is why it is reasonable to make a particular choice. This assessment makes it fair to characterize the view as being concerned with well-being. The view does not make a direct claim about the importance for the rationality of some relationship between the time at which the choice is made, the time of the events being evaluated, and the goals the agent holds at those two times.

I have suggested that, in cases of changing values, the rational choice will often be the one that would maximize the agent's well-being, given the positive response condition. This view may seem to offer a superficial answer to a deep question. Some will feel that a proper answer has to begin from some fundamental stance about the rational significance of time, such as the stances that motivate the prudential solution, the present-aim view, and the simultaneous values view.

Yet it is hard to make these stances fit with modest objectivism. We can recast the views as being about subjective rationality. If we think that there is objective rationality, the views will not answer the most important question about changes in goals—what would it be objectively rational to choose? If we think it is pointless to look for more than an account of what it would be subjectively rational to choose, we will arrive at the present-aim view. However, we are committed to a strong thesis about rationality, and our conclusions about changes in values are wholly explained by this thesis.

A modest conclusion would be that the points made about well-being are relevant to decisions made in the face of conflicts of values over time. But each of the positions about the significance of time faces persuasive counterexamples because all those positions are false. In cases in which a person's values conflict over time, reason does not tell us to rely on our present values, to rely on our future values, or to strike a balance between present values and future values. These stances have seemed reasonable because we have accepted questionable views about reasons or blurred the distinction between objective rationality and subjective rationality.

Chapter 8

Alzheimer's Disease

8.1 DWORKIN'S VIEW

A discussion of the moral claims of the elderly must consider Alzheimer's disease and related diseases that undermine the cognitive abilities and emotional states of their victims. Many of us have a deep fear of suffering that fate ourselves. We see the social importance of the problem as more people live to an age at which those diseases are a serious risk.

Moral philosophers have written about Alzheimer's patients with careful arguments and imagination, although they often reach sharply opposed conclusions. The subject is difficult because we must first address complex factual questions about what capacities these people possess and then face complex ethical questions about how moral principles apply to them.

This chapter will focus on the debate about the moral status of Alzheimer's sufferers. We think that the interests of other people give us reasons to help them. We also believe that the value of autonomy asks us to respect the choices that they are entitled to make about their own lives. In the case of Alzheimer's sufferers, there is disagreement about the nature and importance of the interests they possess and also about whether they are capable of autonomy. I think that even the best discussions of these issues ignore some important considerations in deciding how Alzheimer's patients should be treated.

Like other writers on the subject, I will start from Dworkin's controversial views.[1] I will discuss the objections of two insightful critics of Dworkin, Agnieszka Jaworska, and Seana Shiffrin.[2] These critical discussions motivate my own positive views.

Dworkin believes that sufferers of Alzheimer's disease no longer possess an autonomous will and, in their current state, have only what he calls "experiential" rather than "critical" interests. They have lost the ability to control their lives, and they have also lost their entitlement that their wishes should be respected. He agrees that they make choices and pursue goals of a sort. However, he believes that the cognitive impairments caused by the disease— the destruction of memory, the inability to think reflectively about the past and the future and so the inability to consider their lives as temporal wholes, and the lack of coherence and consistency in their purposes—strip them of the claim to govern their own lives that ordinary people possess.

Dworkin's point about interests concerns the nature of the goods Alzheimer's sufferers are capable of experiencing. They can enjoy what happens during their lives. They might find comfort in the company of a friend or in watching the birds outside their window. Of course their conscious experiences might instead be painful, and they might feel distress from loneliness or confusion. But the person whose experiential life is enjoyable can be said to be

1. Ronald Dworkin, *Life's Dominion* (New York: Alfred A. Knopf, 1993, 218–37).
2. Agnieszka Jaworska, "Respecting the Margins of Agency: Alzheimer's Patients and the Capacity to Value" in *Philosophy & Public Affairs* 28, no. 2, 1999, 105–38; Seana Shiffrin, "Autonomy, Beneficence, and the Permanently Demented" in Justine Burley, ed., *Dworkin and His Critics* (Oxford: Blackwell Publishing, 2004, 195–217). Dworkin replies to Shiffrin in the same volume, 366–70. The challenges to Dworkin's view that I discuss were suggested by these articles but are not strictly speaking identical to either writer's view.

contented and even happy. The contentment is a good for the person who feels it, and Dworkin calls this an experiential interest.

But he thinks Alzheimer's patients are not capable of critical interests. They cannot choose to aim at a goal because they judge it to be important and worthwhile. They cannot pursue a valued project that they identify themselves with and regard as adding value to their lives. If they lack these capacities, then they are incapable of achieving the kind of good that can only come from the pursuit of such projects. Dworkin believes that, for unimpaired people, critical interests are typically more important than experiential interests.

Dworkin may seem committed to the view that our concern for the Alzheimer's patient is exclusively a concern for that person's experiential interests. In furthering that person's experiential interests, we are not constrained by reasons of autonomy.

However, that is not what Dworkin concludes. He looks back to the person before the onset of the disease, when she had both an autonomous will and critical interests. He thinks that each is still in force for her life now, while she is suffering from the disease. Respecting her autonomy now means complying with her wishes as they were then. Some of her past critical interests may extend to the end of her life, if she wished at that earlier time that the rest of her life should go a certain way. We now have a reason to further those critical interests, even if she can no longer understand them. This will best promote the patient's good. So, in another sense, she now possesses both autonomy and critical interests, but they have been inherited from an earlier stage of her life.

These views make Dworkin sympathetic to a conclusion that many find disturbing. Suppose that, at the earlier time, the patient anticipated her decline into dementia and wished that her life should end as quickly as possible once the disease had taken hold. She thought that her life would be better if it ended without a phase of dementia, and this view was the result of reflection and based on convictions that she endorsed as values. Her will and her critical interests each called for life to end. Suppose that, after she has become a victim of Alzheimer's disease, she has contracted another disease that could easily be cured but that would end her life painlessly if it were not cured. The disturbing conclusion is that we should withhold medical treatment of this second disease and allow her to die.

Dworkin does not draw the conclusion that this is the right thing to do or even a permissible thing to do, but he thinks this choice would best express respect for her autonomy and concern for her interests. He suggests that there might be reasons of a different sort that would make it wrong to fail to provide the treatment. However, if we think that the patient's autonomy and the patient's interests are the most important reasons and we agree with Dworkin about their bearing, we will be compelled to accept the disturbing conclusion.

Dworkin thinks that his view applies even if, in her current state, the woman is enjoying her life in the nursing home, eagerly interacts with other people, and seems content. Prolonging her life would promote her experiential interests but frustrate her critical interests, and her critical interests should be viewed as being more important as she held them to be before the disease struck. So, for Dworkin, a peaceful death is the best result for the patient. If her contentment indicates a will to go on living, it is not a will that we are constrained to respect, because she lacks autonomy.

Some find the conclusion morally unconscionable. It asks us to allow someone we could easily save to die, when she is positively responding to her life and not feeling pain or distress. We may feel that this is deeply wrong because of what it means for the patient herself, not for moral reasons of some other kind.

A strong intuitive judgment of this sort carries weight. However, the case presents a dilemma for many of us. It also seems unacceptable to ignore the patient's clearly expressed prior wishes. She considered her future and decided that she wished her life to end rather than to continue in dementia. Presumably we do not think this choice was obviously unreasonable when she made it, and there is no reason to think she would have changed her mind if she were capable of reconsidering the question. Her present contentment is in a sense a product of the harm done by the disease, and we can suppose that it was also something she deplored in advance rather than welcomed. Setting aside her choice might also seem unconscionable.

Given this conflict, the disturbing conclusion cannot simply be dismissed. We might be dissatisfied with it, but we need to find problems in the ideas that led Dworkin to it, and we also need to find a better explanation of what we owe to someone in that condition.

8.2 DWORKIN'S CRITICS

Dworkin's critics see the life and moral claims of the Alzheimer's sufferer very differently. The disease occurs with different degrees of severity, so the disagreement might be explained by generalizing from different cases. Perhaps Dworkin is considering the worst cases, while his critics are thinking about examples in which the damage is less profound. Dworkin does say that a mildly demented person has the capacity for autonomy and the right to exercise it.

However, this assertion does not remove the disagreement. Dworkin thinks his view fits serious but so-called moderate cases of the disease. The patients that he begins by describing do not differ radically from the case studies of Jaworska. Apparently he believes his conclusions apply to the people Jaworska and Shiffrin write about.

The critics see a will that deserves to be respected in many of the patient's actions. Her purposes can be consistent and seriously pursued. She may repeatedly seek out the company of a particular nurse. Her choice is explained by her affection for that person and her desire for affection in return. Her actions are understandable and reasonable given her nature and situation. If she also has some impulses that we cannot begin to understand, that does not justify refusing to take seriously those cases in which we can grasp her purpose.

She might not be capable of considering her life as a whole, deciding that it should have a certain structure and then implementing her choices. To that extent she cannot govern her life in the way that other people can. But this does not mean that she lacks an entitlement to make decisions about matters that her will can encompass. We should see her wishes as giving us reasons to comply with them, reasons that might be outweighed if her wishes were grossly opposed to her own good.

In arguing for his conclusion about autonomy, Dworkin emphasizes what he sees as general problems about her agency. Her goals will typically be inconsistent, there will be no aims that she can persist in pursuing, and her wishes will not reflect any understanding of her own identity. Dworkin thinks she fails a test of minimal competence as an agent, with the result that none of her choices—whether they are bizarre or apparently sensible—should be given the status of exercises of autonomy.

The critics contend that these claims are factually mistaken about many Alzheimer's patients. In many cases, their goals were not inconsistent, and they were capable of pursuing long-term aims. The critics' objections seem to be well taken. Dworkin's claims about autonomy are too strong, but Shiffrin suggests a way of understanding them. Dworkin is motivated by a moral view about autonomy. He thinks that the kind of autonomy that such a person might possess would not have the special value that grounds the moral importance of respecting autonomy.

Dworkin also has an elevated conception of the kind of autonomy that merits protection. Autonomy encompasses the ability to create yourself as a certain kind of person and express your values in the life you live. A patient with moderate to serious Alzheimer's disease is incapable of this (we might struggle to live up to this standard). It is the capacity for this kind of autonomy that is the basis of a strong moral right.

Shiffrin, however, argues that lesser exercises of autonomy also deserve protection. It is ultimately explained by a person's entitlement to determine certain things about his or her own life, and that right is not lost due to cognitive impairment. She points to the right to choose the contents of our own experiences—for example, the right to choose pleasure rather than pain. Making such choices does not structure and organize our lives in the thoroughgoing way that Dworkin envisages, but surely it is something that we are entitled to do. Shiffrin believes that the demented patient clearly has the capacity to exercise autonomy in these humbler ways, and I find her case convincing.

Some find in the Alzheimer's patient a will that her life should continue, and they think this wish is autonomous. This is an important claim to make. It is one thing to credit her with a will to be with a particular person and another thing to credit her with a will to go on living. That her will could have that object could be denied on the grounds that she is not capable of understanding the notions that would form its content: life, death, and the continuation of her own identity. I will suppose that the patient does wish to go on living, although I will not argue for that conclusion. Dworkin himself does not object to saying that the patient has that wish.

With respect to the patient's interests, Dworkin's critics contend that it is also a mistake to see her as capable of no more than hedonic goods and evils located in her experiences. She has the capacity to hold values, and so she has interests that involve her caring for certain things because she regards them as valuable.

When Dworkin argues that Alzheimer's patients do not possess contemporaneous critical interests (as opposed to inherited ones), he says that critical interests must be concerned with a life considered as a temporal whole. But the Alzheimer's patients have no sense of a whole life and so could not evaluate their life as a whole.

Why should this capacity be required? It does not follow that for a concern of mine to count as a critical interest—for example, my concern with writing a poem—I must be capable of thinking about my life as a whole and capable of understanding the difference this accomplishment would make to the overall evaluation of my life. Why is it not enough that the concern should be something I value?

This is Jaworska's criticism of Dworkin. The Alzheimer's sufferer might not be able to think in terms of her complete life, but a critical interest need not have a lifetime as its temporal scope. It suffices if the patient can apply a value to a temporal part of her life.

Jawarska supposes that if a person is capable of valuing something, not merely wanting it, we should credit the person with having a critical interest. So she equates holding a value with having a critical interest. Since she thinks the patients possess some values they thus have critical interests.

The patient's current critical interests will typically be a continuation of some of her previous critical interests since the disease may have erased others from her mind. There is no reason to think their status as values has changed.[3] So benefiting the patient does not just mean providing her with pleasant experiences, and success in achieving her goals is important for her well-being. She has contemporaneous critical interests as well as experiential interests, and some of her current critical interests will support the prolongation of her life.

Jawarska thinks that, if a person is capable of holding a value, the person should be credited with at least a certain amount of autonomy. She might not be able to implement her will by herself, but she has a claim to our help in achieving her goal if the wish is autonomous, and it has the status of a value.

The criticisms of Dworkin seem to lead to conclusions opposite to his. Formerly the patient wanted to die if she declined into senility, but now she has a new will to continue to live. Respecting autonomy tells us to implement her current will, not the will she formerly possessed. Her old critical interests also counted in favor of letting her life end. However, her critical interests have also changed. She no longer endorses the values that led her to that conclusion, and she can no longer even understand them. Her enjoyment of her life signals that she finds value in it. Her new

---

3. It might be argued that her desires do not retain the status of values because she is now incapable of thinking critically and reflectively about them. Valuing is not just making an evaluation as opposed to simply having a preference, it requires being able to think in the appropriate way about values. I will not try to answer this objection, but I think it reads too much into the notion of valuing.

critical interests, along with her experiential interests, support the continuation of her life. If we care about her well-being, we must deal with the interests she has, not the interests she used to have. The two considerations that Dworkin appeals to for not providing medical treatment actually speak in favor of prolonging her life.

However, we are not in a position to draw these conclusions. Even if Dworkin is wrong about the patient's capacities, there are difficult questions to answer before we can decide how she should be treated. What we think about autonomy turns out to differ importantly from what we think about the patient's good.

8.3 AUTONOMY

Suppose we have agreed that the patient now wishes to go on living. Still, her will formerly was that her life should be allowed to end if she arrived at the situation she is now in. There is a conflict between her past will and her present will. Why should we assume that her present will is the one that we should respect? Her previous preference was formed when her faculties were intact and she was capable of understanding the options open to her. Her former will represents the person in her best state; her new will represents her in a damaged and limited condition. Is there not a case for saying that a concern for her autonomy should lead us to respect her past will?

This question should be taken seriously, but I think it can be answered. Its answer depends on the kind of value autonomy is taken to be. We can see this in simpler examples that do not involve dementia. In an ordinary life, a person's will often changes, and sometimes we can see that it has changed for the worse. Their present will might be the result of misplaced emotion, bad reasoning, or a decline in their intelligence.

Nevertheless, the value of autonomy asks us to respect the individual's current will, not what he used to will before he changed his mind. In some cases we might decide not to let him do what he now wants to do if respecting his current will would be radically against his own best interest. But we should not claim that the value of autonomy supports what we are doing. In these cases, autonomy calls for respecting the individual's present will, but it is outweighed by a different consideration. The value of autonomy seems to be naturally present tensed. Respecting people's autonomy means allowing them to act in the way they now choose, not appealing to their past will to compel them to do something they no longer want to do.

Dworkin seemingly explicitly rejects the idea that the value of autonomy is present tensed. He discusses the example of a temporarily deranged Jehovah's Witness who asks for a blood transfusion after an accident. Dworkin says that we should be guided by what he calls the person's "precedent autonomy"—we should respect the person's previous wish never to receive a blood transfusion, not this present wish. He sees this case as being analogous to that of the Alzheimer's sufferer. He describes his own view as being concerned with a person's overall autonomy.[4] This view might suggest that Dworkin thinks we can best respect the patient's autonomy by taking into account the bulk of her wishes over her life as a whole, rather than by simply implementing her present will.

However, the appearance of disagreement is misleading. Dworkin evaluates the Jehovah's Witness case in the way he does

4. "Ronald Dworkin Replies," in *Dworkin and his Critics*, 369.

because he supposes that the derangement means the person's present wish is not an exercise of autonomy. If it were, Dworkin would argue that it should be respected, even if it is less reasonable than his past wish. Precedent autonomy does not mean that a past act of autonomy might carry more weight than a present one, but that if a person, such as the deranged Jehovah's Witness, is now incapable of making an autonomous choice, some prior, noncontemporaneous act of autonomy might still be in force.

These points apply to the Alzheimer's patient. Her new will was formed in circumstances much less favorable for making a reasonable choice, but the content of her new will is not wildly irrational. Given her present life and her own positive response to it, it is not unreasonable for her to prefer that it should continue. In ordinary examples, autonomy calls on us to follow the person's new will, not her old will, even if her new will is less reasonable. The same should be true for the Alzheimer's patient.

It might be the case that complying with the person's new wishes would be against her best interest. I have not yet tried to answer that question, but if that is our reason for ignoring her present will, it is one we regard as outweighing autonomy. In an ordinary case, it would not be a sufficient justification for ignoring the person's autonomy that doing so would benefit her to some degree. We should only set aside her present will if respecting it would be grossly opposed to her best interest. Even if we think that living on is against the best interest of the Alzheimer's patient, it is doubtful whether it should be considered as being extremely destructive of her good.

If the patient has an autonomous wish to live, autonomy supports complying with her current preference. Except in special cases, respecting autonomy, not promoting the patient's best interests, will be the strongest consideration, in agreement with

Dworkin's critics. The best choice would be to provide the life-extending treatment.

8.4 CRITICAL INTERESTS

Dworkin's critics also find new critical interests in the demented patient. Crucially, they do not include her previous critical interest in having her life end without a period of dementia.

They are tempted to conclude that the new critical interests have replaced or superseded her former critical interests. For furthering her good, it is the new critical interests that matter, not the old ones. Since they think her new critical interests include an interest in going on living, continuing to live must be in her best interest overall. Their view of the patient's critical interests resembles the view I argued for in the case of autonomy.

However, they are assimilating the change in the patient's critical interests to the changes in values that occur in ordinary lives. In these cases, the person's critical interests change because she changes her mind about what is worth pursuing. She used to value the challenges of a career, but now she sees more value in family life. She held one evaluative belief, but she changed her mind—perhaps as a result of rational reflection or perhaps not—and adopted a different evaluative belief in its place. In these cases, we think that the new values supersede the old ones. When we consider her good, we think in terms of the values that she holds now.

Some would claim that certain activities are more valuable or worthwhile than others and that the more objective value an activity possesses the more it contributes to the well-being of the person who engages in it. The change in a person's values might be a change from caring about more valuable things to caring about less valuable things. In this case, one determinant of well-being would support treating the person in accordance with her past values and not her present ones. This would have to be balanced against the fact that she will not respond to these values. Sometimes it might be in the person's best interest (although she may not agree) to be treated in accordance with her past critical interests.

This might be the case with people suffering from dementia. Assuming that they are capable of valuing goals, perhaps the things they now care about are less valuable than the things they valued when their minds were whole. In particular, some may think that the preference of the healthy patient to have her life end without a period of dementia is objectively more reasonable than her subsequent wish to have her life continue. If so, they would reject the conclusion of Dworkin's critics about what is in her best interest. But my discussion will not be based on such a claim.

There is a different problem with the view of Dworkin's critics. It is misleading to compare the situation of the Alzheimer's patient to ordinary cases of a change of mind. In one sense, the patient did not change her mind about her past values. She did not reject or abandon her conviction that spending her last years in dementia would make her life worse even if she was contented during those years. She did not change her mind, the disease changed her mind. It stripped her of the ability to even understand her old point of view. Now she can neither assent to nor dissent from her previous conviction.

Because she did not change her mind, it is unclear whether her past critical interests have been superseded. I believe they are still in force, they still apply to her and her life now when she is demented. She cannot consciously endorse them, but that is because she is unable to formulate those thoughts.

This is a different scenario from a genuine change of mind. When a person changes her mind, we give the change great significance, even if she changed her mind for poorly conceived reasons. We would use her new values in deciding what is best for her, despite their tainted history. If we do not do this, it would be because we thought that her new projects had less objective value than her old goals.

Dworkin's critics do not take the absence of a genuine change of mind into account. Jaworska seems to assume that the Alzheimer's patient's new critical interests have supplanted her prior ones so that only the new critical interests are relevant to her present and future good. Jaworska argues that, if the patient counts as having contemporaneous critical interests, then even Dworkin would have to agree that they take precedence over her previous critical interests. This implies that, just because there are new critical interests, the old ones no longer matter.

When Jaworska asks whether we should implement the patient's old values or her new ones, she contends that the demented patient being capable of valuing this choice does not raise problems different from those that would arise in the case of competent people. This viewpoint treats the case of the Alzheimer's patient as an ordinary change of values and neglects the possibility that the way in which the new values replace the old ones might matter as to which choice we should make. She compares the patient who foresees her decline into dementia with a person who anticipates that his ethical values will change for the worse in the future because he will be influenced by conventional opinion, though the comparison does not acknowledge that there is a change of mind in the second case but not the first.

If the patient's old critical interests still have force when she is demented, they are relevant to what is in her best interest during the rest of her life. This is easier to see in an example that does not turn on living versus dying.[5] Suppose that she has been a devout Roman Catholic throughout her life. The disease drove those thoughts and values from her mind. She might now have an interest in attending the bland nondenominational religious services in the nursing home, which she enjoys for the music and the company. Nevertheless, we would appeal to her previous religious convictions, not her current remnants of them, in deciding questions about her funeral. Her life would be better if she were buried according to the practices of her faith, even though in her final years she had lost the ability to understand them. If we draw this conclusion, then we believe that her previous critical interests still matter in deciding what would be best for her now, despite the fact that she no longer consciously adheres to them.

Some will feel that it is a mistake to attribute critical interests to someone who lacks the capacity to understand their content. But compare the case of a person who wishes that his body should not be kept biologically alive after brain death or someone who wishes to be buried with her second husband rather than her first. In these cases, we seem to think that the person's wishes have a claim on us and that the person's life is made better if we fulfill their requests, although these people cannot be said to endorse those wishes at the time when they are carried out. Why not think the same about the prior critical interests of the Alzheimer's patient? Her wishes still have force because she never changed her mind about them.[6]

The reply might be that the case of the Alzheimer's patient is different precisely because she still exists at the time at which her

---

5. This example was suggested by one of Jaworska's case studies.
6. Dworkin uses similar comparisons to support his view of the importance of the Alzheimer's patient's prior critical interests (*Life's Dominion*, 228). Jaworska agrees that, in principle, critical interests can still apply to the life of a person who is incapable of understanding them, is unconscious, or has already died (111).

previous wishes would be carried out and at that time she has different wishes. The conclusion it supports is that we must also take her new values into account. It is not a reason for thinking that her old wishes are now irrelevant.

I am not denying that the patient also has new critical interests that matter in determining her good and that those interests might support prolonging her life. I think both sets of critical interests apply to her life now, and they conflict. This position differs from Dworkin's view that the only critical interests the patient possesses are the so-called old ones and the apparent view of his critics that those interests have been supplanted and only the new ones matter.

How should the conflict be resolved? The patient's own view, when she had all of her faculties, would have been that her old critical interests counted for more than her new interests and current experiential interests. The onset of dementia did not involve her changing her mind about their relative importance. This may not settle the question of what would be best for her now, but we would need to have strong reasons before concluding that going on living was in her best interest overall.[7]

There is another reason why the prior critical interests would be stronger. They include a view about the overall structure that her life should have, expressed in her directive about how she should

---

7. Shiffrin makes an important point about Dworkin's view (200, 210). Suppose the patient's prior wish had instead been that her life should be prolonged for as long as possible after she had become demented, even if she was suffering horribly. We would be unwilling to prolong the misery of someone who cannot understand what is happening to her. But if we agree with Dworkin's conclusion about the original case, we might be forced to accept this consequence. If the patient's prior critical interests win out in the case in which she wants her life to end, it seems they should also win out in the case in which she wants her life to continue despite the suffering. This is a problem for Dworkin, but the view I have explained can avoid this problem as it actually is in the patient's best interest to live on, despite the pain, if that is what her prior critical interests call for. However, when we turn to the issue of autonomy presumably it is clear that when she is suffering her will is that the suffering should end. Given the terms of the example, the

be treated if she became demented. The demented patient has a desire to go on living, and this desire has the status of a critical interest. Still, it is not an interest of exactly the same sort. It does not express a new view about the overall shape of her life, since she can no longer think in the way that is necessary to form such a view. About questions concerning the overall shape of her life, there is only one view to consider, the view that was one of her prior critical interests. This is an important interest to have satisfied, because it is connected with having the maximum amount of control over one's life. It conflicts with the demented patient's new critical interest in continuing to live, but this prior critical interest might be thought more important than the new one.

Just as the patient does not self-consciously change her mind about values, she also does not deliberately transform her will from her first wish to die quickly into a new wish to continue to live. If there is no change of will in that sense, why should we not draw the same conclusion about autonomy that I have drawn about the patient's interests—because her prior will was never withdrawn, it, too, has force for the rest of her life? It must be taken into account along with her current will in deciding how best to respect her autonomy. My answer must appeal to the view that autonomy is present tensed. She now wishes to live, and we cannot respect her autonomy by allowing her to die when that will is firmly in place. The assertion that autonomy is present tensed might seem to beg the question. I have not given general arguments that autonomy is present tensed (I am not sure what arguments could be offered), but I think that our judgments about particular examples support that view.

only way to respect her will is not to treat the disease so that her life ends. This is a case in which respecting autonomy leads us to reasonably act against her best interest.

8.5 A DIFFERENT APPROACH

I will briefly consider a different approach to these issues. One important question is, What would be in the patient's best interest? The various views about experiential interests and critical interests that I have already discussed are attempts to answer that question. I have assumed that this question is equivalent to considerations of what would make her complete life best overall. However, some feel that in considering the interests of the Alzheimer's patient, it is almost as though we are forced to choose between the goods of two distinct people: the healthy person before the disease (P1) and the person after the state of dementia is in place (P2). They are confident about what would be best for P1 (an early death for P2, in virtue of P1's deeply held critical interests) and equally confident about what would be best for P2 (more of P2's happy existence). But if we ask, "What would be in the overall best interest of person P, a lifetime that ends when dementia begins or a lifetime that includes a final stage of dementia and contentment?" some critics might deny that this question has an answer.

This view would be inescapable if dementia breached personal identity, so that it was a mistake to say that P1 was one and the same person as P2. In that case, we would agree that, in deciding how to treat P2, we should look to her interests and her will rather than to the prior interests and wishes of P1.[8] However, most people do not think that dementia destroys personal identity, except perhaps in the final and most terrible stages of the disease.

---

8. Rebecca Dresser denies that the demented patient is identical to the person before the illness, and she draws this conclusion about how the patient should be treated. See "Life, Death, and Incompetent Patients: Conceptual Infirmities and Hidden Values in the Law," *Arizona Law Review* 28, 1986, 373–405.

A weaker view of the same sort would hold that, even if personal identity is preserved, identity might not be what matters most in applying the moral notions of a person's good and autonomy. Some philosophical theories of personal identity maintain that what matters are relations of psychological continuity and connectedness, supposedly the facts in which identity consists. Even if we do not agree that these psychological relations constitute personal identity, we might think that the relations are important for their own sake in applying those moral concepts. Dementia clearly involves a significant weakening of these relations, a reality that could influence what we say about the patient's good and autonomy. In chapter 6, I discussed versions of these views, applied to elderly people who are not suffering from dementia.

Certainly there is much less psychological continuity in the lifetime of the person whose life ends in moderate or extreme Alzheimer's disease than in a lifetime without the disease. But it is not clear that the difference is enough to undermine applying those moral concepts in the ordinary way—that is, in the way they would be applied to a person whose life contained the normal amount of psychological continuity over time. The lives of Alzheimer's patients can contain significant psychological continuity in terms of character, desires, and personality traits even if there are striking gaps in memory.[9] So we should be cautious before deciding that the interests of P1 are irrelevant to the good of P2 or before concluding that there is no answer to the question of what would make the patient's lifetime as a whole better or worse.

Nevertheless, if we did think in terms of what I call the two goods view, what implications would it have? Shiffrin thinks that, in virtue of the weakness of the psychological connections

---

9. Jaworska's case studies seem to bear this out.

between P1 and P2, it is questionable whether we should allow the autonomous choices and critical interests of P1 any role in determining the fate of P2. She might say that the weakening of psychological continuity is itself a strong reason for thinking that those interests do not apply to the patient's present life. I am not convinced that the extent of the breakdown in psychological connections would justify that conclusion but whether or not we agree, we expect the two goods approach to lead in this direction. Since we are making a choice about P2, it is the good of P2, not the good of P1, that should matter.

However, Jeff McMahan uses the two goods view to support the opposite conclusion.[10] He thinks that we can decide which of the two lifetimes would be best for the person. The shorter life without dementia would be better. But he also thinks there is a conflict between what would be best for the person's complete life and what would be best for the patient now, when she is demented. The weakening of psychological continuity isolates the demented patient from her prior critical interests. The disease has fundamentally changed her nature, and her current good depends on her present interests. It might be better to simply promote her present and future good. McMahan seems to be leaning toward a conclusion like Shiffrin's.

However, McMahan thinks that, before we decide to prolong the patient's life, we must weigh the person's present and future good against her good at the time before the illness harmed her. He argues that the contribution made to the good of P1 by implementing her wish not to prolong her life would be greater than the

10. Jeff McMahan, *The Ethics of Killing* (New York: Oxford University Press, 2002, 496–504). McMahan does not discuss autonomy, perhaps because he thinks that the only autonomous will is to be found in the patient before the disease.

contribution made to the good of P2 by implementing her wish to continue living. So Dworkin's conclusion turns out to be right, although not for the reasons Dworkin gives. The two goods model separates the good of P1 and the good of P2, and the good of P1 outweighs the good of P2.

I am not sure that the case is convincing. McMahan points out that most of the person's life was lived before the onset of the disease and that during this period the person was at her best, with her faculties intact. This is true, but it does not show that P1 has more at stake in the choice than P2. He says that P2 could not realize much good if her life were to continue. Dementia will prevent her from enjoying the most important goods. Her final years will lack unity. We may find these points persuasive (although McMahan might be exaggerating the disconnected nature of the person's life in moderate cases of dementia), but they will not justify his conclusion until we have compared the good of P2 with the good of P1.

One problem for McMahan's view comes from his own appeal to the weakened psychological connections between P1 and P2. This is his reason for thinking that the person's earlier critical interests do not make it in P2's interest that her life should end. But the isolating effect should work in both directions. The weakened psychological connections should also reduce the harm that will be done to the good of P1 if P2 lives on.

McMahan thinks the harm done by extending P2's life is suffered by the person before the disease strikes, that is, we should locate the harm temporally earlier in the person's life, so the harm is suffered by P1. The dementia experienced by P2 has the effect of reducing the value of the life that P1 has already lived. P1 had goals about how her life should end, and if P2 continues to live in dementia, P1's goals will be frustrated rather than fulfilled.

Yet even if we think about the good of P1 in this way, it is not clear how much this will harm P1. The only critical interest of P1 that would be frustrated by a longer life for P2 is her interest in the way that P's life will end. In this case, the ending that she wishes to avoid would be separated from P1 by the weakening of psychological continuity. We might decide to count the frustration of this interest as a serious harm to P1, but does preventing this harm to P1 justify allowing P2 to die, when P2 would benefit from a longer life?

A strict version of the two goods view might not result in allowing P2 to die. The two goods view takes as its model cases involving two different people. In such cases, we would not refuse to provide life-extending medical treatment to one person merely because that would result in a greater amount of good for someone else whose life was not at stake.

We could reach McMahan's final conclusion if we think that, because the Alzheimer's patient did not abandon her previous critical interests, they apply to P2 and not just to P1. But if we make this claim, we are abandoning the two goods view.

My conclusions fall between those of Dworkin and his critics. If we can discern a will to go on living in the Alzheimer's patient, we should provide the life-extending treatment, despite the patient's clear prior wishes. Although I have not argued for it, such a will is present in many who suffer from the disease. With respect to the patient's interests, it is best that her life should end. If we consider the two possible lifetimes—a shorter life that ends soon after dementia begins and a longer life with an extended period of dementia—the first life is the better one to have lived, given the patient's prior critical interests.

Our choice involves a conflict between respecting the patient's autonomy and promoting her good. The conflict should be resolved in favor of autonomy, since the continuation of her life will not have disastrous consequences for the quality or value of her life. What we say about autonomy and what we say about the person's good might diverge, and in considering the patient's critical interests, it is important to distinguish between a genuine change of mind value and the changes in the patient's mind caused by the disease.

Despite their confusion and frequent incoherence, Alzheimer's patients can be committed to values. They possess a will that can be steadily directed at certain aspects of their own lives and that deserves our respect.

Their will might take a different direction than it did before the disease, and significant differences in what they value might emerge. The differences might be over trivial matters, but they might instead concern such fundamental questions as whether their lives should continue.

Our first reaction might be that we must be concerned with their current wishes and values. To help them exercise what control they can over their lives, we must address their current will, and to benefit them we must work with their current values.

I think the first reaction is right in terms of autonomy, but in the case of the patient's good, the change is at best a borderline case of a change in values. The patients' values are different now, but they did not change their minds. The difference between what they value now and what they valued before is explained by the disease. The patient did not abandon her previous values. Her view of her good was never retracted, and it continues to shape what is good for her now.

Chapter 9

Conclusion

9.1 JUSTICE FOR AGE GROUPS

In our lives, we pass through the temporal stages of youth, maturity, and old age, belonging in turn to each of the age groups that those stages define. We are born at different times, so we can also be grouped into different generations or birth-cohorts. We remain members of the same generation throughout the different temporal stages of our lives. These simple truths provide a complicated field for the application of principles of justice.

There are some familiar principles of justice that will hold between individuals, at least if they belong to the same society and live under common institutions. They will hold between exact contemporaries, and they should also hold between the individuals who constitute a particular generation and the members of a different generation that temporally overlaps with the first one. For example, they will hold between a given generation and the generation of its children or the generation of its parents. Problems that arise in deciding whether they also hold, or some other principles hold, between people whose lives are separated by centuries should not make us lose sight of this.

Rawls's principles of justice seem to be designed for this role. Principles of this sort tend to be given the temporal scope of complete lives. The principles tell us something about what the members of one generation owe to the members of an adjoining generation. I have tried to avoid assumptions about the content of the principles concerned with complete lives because I hope that my discussion can offer something useful even to people who disagree about the nature of this kind of justice. More importantly, I want to concentrate on the less well-understood ideas about justice that are specific to relations between different generations and age groups.

I have argued for a positive account of what those principles are, claiming that they apply the egalitarian value of priority to temporal parts of lives rather than to complete lives. This bald statement of the view does not reveal claims that the view contains. The view is intended to be egalitarian in a broad sense, although I did not attempt to make a general case that egalitarianism is an essential part of a reasonable theory of justice. I did appeal to intuitive judgments about distribution between age groups that seem to be best explained by egalitarian principles. I also pointed out that such institutions as social security systems that distribute among age groups often contain an element of egalitarianism in their policies.

Egalitarianism is not the only moral value relevant to justice between age groups. Such values as promoting the general good and desert are also found in those institutions, and moral theory might well give a significant role to these values in understanding this part of justice.[1] I emphasized egalitarianism because I thought I had something new to say about it and because I believe egalitarianism is especially relevant to some of the hardest questions

---

1. Egalitarian writers are often hostile to the value of desert. This is best illustrated by Rawls's dismissal of noninstitutional desert. They see desert as a rival to their own distributive principle. So many egalitarians claim that desert is not a legitimate value at all.

about the treatment of the elderly, for example, in the case of the miserable lives of some elderly people with physical and mental impairments. But fairness between age groups is not exclusively concerned with responding to extreme hardship experienced by the very old, and in many other cases other values might be the most important factors.

Intuitive judgments provided my reasons for thinking that the element of egalitarianism in this kind of justice is not exclusively supplied by egalitarian principles concerned with lifetimes. Those judgments motivate the application of egalitarian values to temporal parts of lives, and this distinguishes the view from more familiar egalitarian accounts of justice dealing with complete lives. But the case did not only appeal to intuitive judgments. I tried to answer the reasons for thinking that egalitarian principles can only be applied to lifetimes. If there are no fundamental problems with the application, it is reasonable to adopt it.

Another stage in the theory is the attempt to decide which egalitarian value should be applied to temporal parts of lives. The decision to apply some egalitarian value in that way is the most crucial element. In previous chapters, I argued that priority was better suited to this role than equality, but the reasons I gave were not decisive. I would not complain if others chose equality or

---

While I cannot defend what I say here, I do not share this attitude. Egalitarianism and desert views compete for the same moral territory—they are rival theories of distributive justice. But both theories express legitimate claims of fairness. A badly off person who is lazy and mildly dishonest can, nevertheless, have a claim to a job because he is badly off, while a second person who is already successful can have a claim to the same position on the basis of merit. This claim exists even if the successful person had important advantages in his upbringing that the first person lacked through no fault of his own. This history might mean the first person should not be disadvantaged by things that were not his fault, and this is why we should see him as having an egalitarian claim. But the history does nothing to undermine the claim of a different sort that the second person possesses. We should take both claims into account, even though they conflict.

sufficiency. I do not agree with these conclusions, but I see them as fitting the general form of the view that I have defended.

The claim that priority can be applied to temporal parts of lives is a simple idea. It does most of the work in my account.

The basic idea has no special connection with age. The view would often ask us to help people who are old, but it does not help them because they are old. It helps them because they are badly off. The view calls for making exactly the same judgment about a young person with the same level of well-being. The idea is the key to understanding a supposedly elusive kind of justice, justice between age groups as opposed to justice between generations and as opposed to justice between exact contemporaries. But the basic idea has no special connection to classifications in terms of age groups or generations. The basic idea would function in the same way if the world never contained people of different ages, if everyone was born on the same day and, after 50 years, died on the same day so that people never differed in age. In this case, we could still apply priority to temporal parts of lives. I have already explained the implications of applying priority in the same way inside and across lives and across different times. The view does not give intrinsic moral importance to facts about time.

Given the limited resources of the view, people will feel that it cannot give adequate explanations of what I am trying to explain. Something more—a view that gives moral importance to facts about time, questions the significance of personal identity, or appeals to a moral value that is uniquely connected to age groups must be part of the story.

The only answer to this criticism is to show that the basic idea provides a satisfactory explanation, and the additional ideas are not needed. I have tried to do that in the preceding chapters of this book.

Identifying the basic idea with justice between age groups needs further comment. It is, in part, terminological legislation on my part. Principles of priority or equality concerned with complete lives will also be relevant to distribution among people of different ages. I have labeled them as principles of justice for generations, but we could also consider them as additional principles of justice for age groups. What matters is the difference between principles with the temporal scope of a lifetime and principles that deal with people at particular times, not choosing between generation and age group when searching for names for the principles. The difference between age groups and generations is clear, as is the difference between the two kinds of principle but not the appropriateness of using those names for the two kinds of principle.

However, I think the legislation has some value. Egalitarian principles concerned with lifetimes are not puzzling. Egalitarian principles concerned with people at particular times are puzzling. That is why we have to give reasons for thinking that we need these principles and respond to criticisms of them. This book began with puzzles about justice between the young and the old. I think that the solution to those puzzles requires principles with limited temporal scope. We are puzzled because we do not naturally think in terms of such principles. Since the principles remove the puzzle, it is helpful to give them special status by calling them principles of justice for age groups.

9.2 THE RELEVANT REASONS

Thinking about the institutions that transfer resources across age groups and generations can help to discover the different kinds of moral reasons we need to distinguish. In our society, public institutions that transfer resources across generations are fundamentally important. They collect and distribute more resources and have a greater effect on the economy than welfare programs unrelated to age. Understandably, one desirable objective of these institutions is to promote the goal prudential saving.

Viewing social security as a mandatory savings program, it should be structured in a way that makes our lives go best overall, if we consider those lives as temporal wholes and take into account contributions made early in life and benefits received after retirement. We want the transfers that the institution enforces to do more good than harm in terms of the lives of the people that they influence. We also want almost all individuals to benefit in the long run from their participation in the programs when we look at their complete lifetimes. One simple notion of being benefited by the institution is that the sacrifices we make when young for the sake of others should be smaller than the benefits we eventually receive when we are old.

Resources should be transferred between different temporal stages of the same life and between different temporal stages of different lives in the way that will maximize the total amount of well-being that peoples' complete lives contain. This idea is shared by the traditional conception of prudence as individual rationality and by a utilitarian assessment of institutions such as social security.

However, the existence of these institutions reveals some additional concerns of fairness. Given that the state is intervening to take resources away from some to give to others, that participation by individuals in the institution is mandatory, and that the purpose of these institutions is precisely to transfer resources between generations (this is true of social security, although not of health care), it is important that they should treat different generations fairly or equitably in the course of achieving their goals.

I explained this kind of fairness as requiring rough equality in what different generations gain and lose through the operation of the institutions. This is a limited kind of fairness under an institution, as opposed to a more general kind of justice that would look to the overall quality of people's lives and put constraints on how those institutions operate—for example, by allowing the people whose lives as a whole would be worst to benefit more from these institutions than others. Justice under the institution is concerned with complete lifetimes.

A final kind of justice is the most difficult to understand, and my theory attempts to explain it. It is what we usually have in mind when we think about justice between the young and the old and is obvious in the history of the institutions themselves, since they were not created simply to compel us to save prudently. They were also intended to support us during a specific temporal stage of life, old age. The institutions embody the view that the elderly have a claim to support from the members of other age groups and that a significant violation of this claim can be an injustice. This concern can appropriately be identified as one of justice between age groups rather than justice between generations, because it directly governs the synchronic distribution of resources between people of different ages.

The distinctive and philosophically puzzling feature about this concern is the focus on temporal parts of lives rather than complete lives. Understanding the concern requires thinking in a way that is nontraditional when it comes to philosophical theories of justice. Perhaps this helps to create the appearance that the moral concern is irreducibly concerned with age groups themselves. If we assume that the moral claims of individuals must be based on complete lives, we might think that these claims must be held by subjects other than individuals, perhaps age groups themselves.

However, this concern is best explained by the moral claims of individuals, claims that they have in virtue of the quality of temporal parts of their lives rather than in virtue of the quality of their complete lives. These claims are discovered by comparing temporal stages in different lives, not by thinking diachronically about the different temporal stages in a single life. Rather than applying prudence, we should apply some ethical value concerned with interpersonal justice. This kind of justice aims at equality among the simultaneous temporal parts of different lives, or it gives priority to improving the worst temporal parts of lives. The claims can be most convincingly based on the value of priority.

It may seem strange that I have made substantive egalitarian claims about justice between the temporal parts of lives while trying to avoid similar claims about justice between complete lives. However, I think that claims of the first sort are required to understand the rationale for social security. I have tried to make the claims as uncontroversial as possible—there should not be extreme inequality between the young and the old, or we should attach at least some priority to helping the worst off among the elderly. Similar claims made about complete lives would be just as persuasive, but they are not essential for understanding the basis of social security transfers.

My assertion that this consideration is part of the history of social security will not convince everyone that we have an independent moral concern with temporal parts of lives.

So I have argued against other ways of trying to explain the judgments that I think this concern accounts for. I have argued that the reasonable conclusions about what we owe to the elderly cannot be understood as an application of utilitarianism, as a matter of helping the people who need help the most. Our concern for the elderly is not simply utilitarian because it leads us to give them more than utilitarianism would assign to them. If they are sufficiently worse off than others, then considerations of justice provide a reason for helping them, even if we could help younger and better-off people more. If we consider the condition of the lives of people who are very old—especially with respect to the provision of medical care—such a case is far more than a theoretical possibility.[2]

I have also criticized Daniels's theory that attempts to understand the claims of the elderly in a different way. Daniels agrees that there is a distinctive kind of justice that deserves to be called justice between age groups. He agrees that the principles of this kind of justice are distinct from principles of justice dealing with complete lives. He believes that there can be unfairness that is specifically concerned with how people fare during temporal parts of their lives.

These claims are central to my own view, but Daniels thinks that our concern with stages of lives is ultimately explained by a deeper concern with lifetimes. We discover principles of justice for age groups by thinking about complete lives and applying prudential rationality.

Instead we should understand these claims as being concerned with parts of lives at the deepest level. These claims apply an interpersonal value to the temporal stages of different lives, not the notion of prudence. In chapter 5, I suggested that the best explanation of the claims is the value of priority applied to people at times. In chapter 6, I suggested that we should revise the traditional conception of prudence so that it grants this priority,

2. I have not explicitly considered the view that whatever claims the elderly might possess are fully explained by one kind of desert. This view contends that the strength of those claims depend on the contributions that they have made in the past to institutions such as social security or, more generally, on their overall contributions to other people and society. However, the view cannot explain all that we owe to those who are old and living miserable lives.

by denying that prudence has the goal of maximizing the total amount of well-being in a complete life. As a result, an application of priority across lives and an application of prudence inside lives will lead to the same conclusions, as Daniels thinks. But the priority view ultimately explains some features of prudential thinking and the conclusions that prudence draws about lifetimes, not the other way around.

Some will feel that my conclusions only make sense if we suppose that, in old age, I will be a different person than I now am. I have resisted this interpretation (see chapter 7). The conclusions that I have drawn about the treatment of the elderly could be explained by a revisionist view of personal identity. But this explanation would compel us to accept conclusions that seem unreasonable. The extra layer of explanation is unnecessary. The conclusions have an adequate ethical explanation.

I have not attempted to compare the strengths of the different kinds of moral reason that I have described. Justice under institutions is important because of the significance of the institutions in question. The reasons described in chapter 6 are one part of a general theory of justice, but that does not guarantee that they will always be stronger than considerations about justice under institutions. People's interest in prudential saving can justify some inequalities between age groups and generations.

My most important conclusion is that judging the fairness of social security involves moral complexity. We need to take into account, compare, and weigh reasons of fundamentally different kinds. The conclusion may seem banal, but I think it is significant because many views, both in the theory of justice and public debates about social security, deny this complexity.

Daniels contends that justice between age groups does not involve genuine competition between the moral claims of different people, the young and the old.

Other writers think in a similar way. If we think diachronically in terms of the complete life course, the appearance of difficult issues about justice is dispelled. Since the appearance of conflicting claims of justice is superficial, the way is clear to concentrate on the task of designing social security to function in the most economically efficient way as a form of saving.

These claims play an unfortunate role in the public debate. They imply that there cannot be a conflict between maximally efficient saving and meeting claims of justice specific to the elderly. They equate the savings function of social security represented by the lifetime perspective good and its goal of fairness to the elderly represented by synchronic constraints on distribution between age groups. This makes some think that, if social security works as an efficient form of saving, it cannot be subject to any serious moral criticism.

It is important to try to design the system of transfers so that it will work to almost everyone's advantage. But this does not justify denying that the subject involves serious and complex issues of interpersonal justice. Even if the system tends to benefit everyone as it is applied consistently through time, maintaining it can make significantly different demands on different generations. Adjusting contributions and benefits will involve gains for some and losses for others. If we respond to a financial problem by maintaining contributions at their current level and by reducing the size of benefits, those who are old when the change is made will lose and will not be compensated for their loss.

If I am right about the final kind of justice, respecting the claims of the elderly might involve real sacrifices by others. Since this kind of fairness is explained by giving priority to the badly off, it can conflict with the goal of making our lifetimes contain as much well-being as possible. A social security system that increases the total amount of happiness in an average life might still fail to give the elderly what they have a claim to possess. They can have a claim to certain kinds of health care even though that is not the most efficient way of using resources.

Because different reasons are relevant, it might sometimes be fair to increase the inequality among people's complete lives. In other cases, it will be right to accept inequality among age groups in order to prevent inequality among the complete lives of the members of different generations. We might be justified in not helping the worst off among the elderly now if this would create too great a difference between their lifetimes and the lives of others. These choices will not be easy to make. We should admit that it requires deciding a question about how best to realize justice, given competition among the claims of different people.

9.3 AGE GROUPS AND GENERATIONS

The views that I have criticized simplify the issues about generations and age groups and then suggest that they are easily resolved. By contrast, it is sometimes claimed that these issues are irresolvable.

Peter Laslett stresses the difficulty of generational justice.[3] He thinks the subject will remain murky because we do not understand what birth-cohorts and age groups are. Generations have a

---

3. Peter Lasett, "Is There a Generational Contract" in *Justice between Age Groups and Generations,* Peter Lasett, ed. (New Haven, CT: Yale University Press, 1992, 45–46).

"processional" nature. They are separated and distinguished by the passage of time, but no generation is ever fully and uniquely present at any given time. The population of a society at a particular time will never consist of all and only the members of one generation. If we cannot understand generations, we cannot determine what counts as justice between them.

Vern Bengtson and Tonya Murray believe that acceptable ideas about generational justice cannot be set out in terms of general principles.[4] We must take into account the complex historical experiences of different birth-cohorts. They suggest we have little choice but to use the norms about generational justice that those birth-cohorts accept.

The historian Andrew Achenbaum agrees in emphasizing the difficulty of demarcating generations.[5] He finds philosophical theories of justice unhelpful when applied to generations and age groups. The best we can do is to maintain the values accepted by the founders of social security, perhaps with some modest reforms in response to changing social and economic circumstances.

I suspect that these writers are in part mistaking the moral complexity that I have described for the different condition of being intractable to reflective ethical thought. The pessimists stress what they think of as the puzzling nature of generations and age groups themselves. The boundary between one generation and another or one age group and another is vague. Different cultures seem to understand and identify generations and age groups in different ways. For some, the notion of a generation

4. Vernon Bengtson and Tonya Murray, "'Justice' Across Generations (and Cohorts)" in *Justice Across Generations: What Does It Mean?* Lee M. Cohen, ed. (Public Policy Institute, AARP, 1993, 111–38).

5. Andrew Achenbaum, "Social Security's Three R's" in *Social Security—The First Half-Century,* Gerald Nash, Noel Pugach, and Richard Tomasson, eds. (Albuquerque: University of New Mexico Press, 1988).

retains a strong link to the parent-child relationship. So they might think that, for two generations to be distinct, there should be an age difference of at least 20 years between them. Other societies might individuate generations in terms of supposedly significant political or cultural events. In North America, many people would think that there is a deep generational difference between people who graduated from university in 1963 and those who graduated in 1970, even though there is no possibility of a parent-child connection between these two groups. Cultures that think about generations in this way would see different political or cultural changes as marking generational differences. An event such as the assassination of President John Kennedy, a significant generational signpost for many of us, would not be of much value in understanding the relationships between people of different ages in central Africa.

If all of these variations could somehow be sorted out, we would still need to decide what the boundary of a generation should be. Does each individual belong to one and only one generation? What criteria could we use to draw these sharp boundaries?

Different societies also differ in the significance that they attach to these classifications. Arguably, some do not think in these terms at all. In our own culture, we are prone to think in terms of generations and age groups in political, economic, and cultural contexts, often in a discriminating way. In a more static culture, there would be less of a need to think about differences between generations or perhaps less reason to even have the concept of a generation at all.

The points I have made about generations can be replicated in the case of age groups. All cultures will recognize a difference between childhood and maturity and notice the importance of natural processes of aging. But different societies will divide lives into significant temporal stages in different ways. These differences will reflect other differences between those cultures, such as the average lifespan, the institutions of marriage and the family, and the nature of the economy and culture. It would be just as difficult to propose sharp criteria for individual membership of age groups as in the case of generations, even if we could reach agreement about what the significant age groups were.

If we think that principles of justice must deal with generations and age groups as such, there will be other difficult questions that must be answered. We might have to decide whether an individual's continuing membership in a particular generation is a more fundamental fact about that person than his current membership in a particular age group. Are the characteristics of so-called Baby Boomers best explained by their constituting a distinct birth-cohort, or are they best understood in terms of the characteristic attitudes of middle age?

However, if I am right, these concerns cannot be difficulties of principle, and they do not justify giving up on moral thinking. All of the relevant reasons are, in the end, attached to individuals, not age groups or generations. Indeterminacy in identifying generations and age groups is not a fundamental obstacle, although it might be a problem in practically designing social security institutions (for example, in setting ages of eligibility). In principle, we could state the reasons that I have explained without reference to age groups and generations.

Suppose that a particular culture does not think in terms of generations or age groups, at least not to a significant degree. Differences between parents and children in attitudes, values, and behavior do not seem especially important, so parents and children are not considered collectively as forming two distinct generations. In considering a life, there is only a rough distinction among childhood, maturity, and old age.

Suppose also that I am right in suggesting that the notion of egalitarian priority can be reasonably applied to people at times as well as to lifetimes. Then the kind of moral reasons that I describe in chapters 5 and 6 will be present in this culture, whether or not its members act in accordance with those reasons or acknowledge them. It will still be true that well-being matters in the particular way that this version of the priority view claims. The fact that the people that I have imagined do not think explicitly in terms of generations and age groups does not mean that the reasons do not exist.

9.4 SOCIAL SECURITY

I have not offered an answer to the debate about whether social security should be maintained roughly in its present form or radically restructured. Perhaps that is not surprising for a book about moral philosophy. I have criticized some positions in the debate that ignore relevant reasons. In virtue of the moral complexity I have described, we should not rush to conclusions about the institutional form that social security should take.

The reluctance to draw conclusions is not just a consequence of the fact that I have not seriously attempted to weigh the different kinds of moral reason against one another. Even if we could make confident judgments of the relative strength of the reasons, strong conclusions would not be justified. Moving from the moral considerations to specific conclusions about the institution would involve economic, sociological, and political questions.

Given the difference between the goal of social security as economically efficient saving and the goal of fairness to the elderly as an age group, we cannot simply dismiss the view that they should be served by different policies rather than being combined in a single program. One possibility would be to separate a needs-based welfare program aimed specifically at the elderly from a more general system of saving for retirement that might continue to work through payroll deductions. Since the two goals are significantly different, it may be less effective to pursue them both through the same institution with a single source of revenue and a single system for distributing revenue once it has been collected.

Strong practical reasons against this suggestion, however, may arise. Some would argue that the separation of the two programs would tend to undermine political support for the needs-based program on the part of well-off citizens who would not benefit from it. Such arguments are often used by defenders of traditional social security programs and vigorously resisted by those campaigning for radical changes in the institution.

Whether they are good or bad, these arguments are not to be assessed by moral philosophy. The proposal may be mistaken, but there is no objection to it based simply on the nature of the relevant moral reasons. I suspect that a number of different institutional structures could adequately respond to the moral reasons that I have described. The choice between them will depend on economic, sociological, and historical factors and will not be a direct consequence of principles of justice.

This chapter has emphasized the limited but important role of the ideas that I have explained in debates about the public institutions. It is equally important to place those ideas in the context of moral philosophy and in the broader context of reflective thought about principles of justice. For the issues I am discussing, the most important task of ethical thought is to properly relate values and principles to fundamental facts about time and temporally extended human lives. This goal is at the heart of this book. The difficulty of achieving it helps to explain the puzzlement and disagreement that we encounter.

One response to those fundamental facts is to assert the dominance of the lifetime perspective and claim that the values in question can only be applied to complete lives. This seems to be the response of most egalitarian writers and nonegalitarian ones as well. Obviously there are powerful reasons supporting it. I have suggested that this response cannot avoid marginalizing justice between the young and the old. We cannot think exclusively in terms of lifetimes and also recognize fairness between age groups as a substantive matter of interpersonal justice in its own right. I also claimed that the arguments in its favor can be answered. I have tried to make this response seem counterintuitive when we apply it to particular cases.

A second fundamental response is the appeal to prudence. This position takes the lifetime perspective as fundamental but gives partial recognition to fairness between the young and the old by treating distribution between the temporal parts of different lives as morally equivalent to a prudential distribution over the different temporal stages of one life. This response is adopted by a number of writers. Undeniably, there is something appealing about the thought that what we owe to the elderly is simply what an intelligent and prudent person would choose to provide for her own old age viewing it in the context of her life as a whole.

I suspect this response is adopted because of its appearance of simplicity, precision, and its apparent fit with other persuasive ideas, for example, the rationality of prudence and the importance of the lifetime perspective.

My main criticism has been to try to show that the appeal to prudence leads to unacceptable conclusions. My second argument was to explain a persuasive alternative view of the application of values to our lives, one that is not committed to the same disturbing consequences.

I have proposed that the claims stemming from the temporal stages in lives include some that are a matter of applying an ordinary ethical value, such as equality or priority for the badly off, to people at particular times. In the case of equality, these claims will lead to very different conclusions than the appeal to prudence. In the case of priority, my view will also differ from the appeal to prudence it generates, as long as prudence is interpreted as a maximizing notion.

These views raise issues about the importance of time and the importance of facts about the timing of the good and bad events that impact on our lives. The most plausible way of applying equality to people at times—the simultaneous segments view—involves giving intrinsic importance to the fact of simultaneity, and this is a reason for finding it implausible. However, the simultaneous segments view does not make time matter in a way that would contradict the concern for temporal neutrality and the avoidance of pure time biases that are part of the traditional way of understanding prudence.

The best way of understanding the priority view does not give intrinsic importance to facts about timing. It is best to interpret prudential rationality as including priority.

Applying these values to temporal stages in different lives does not automatically bring with it the application of values inside a life. However, I have independently argued that, in the case of priority, it is reasonable to apply the value inside a life. The application is not motivated by a special way of thinking of a person's life through time but by the best way of understanding the value of priority itself; the special significance of a benefit received when a person is badly off applies in intrapersonal cases as well as interpersonal cases.

This book should end by returning to the elderly. The values I applied to them can also be applied to others, and I did not intend to argue that the elderly should be privileged when compared to others or to rest a case on sentiment. However, the idea for this book came from thinking that certain moral values had a special application to the problems of the elderly and it is with this particular group that I have found the place to work the ideas out. I have tried to remember their circumstances even when thinking about complex principles. It is no longer true that age means misery, but many people are living under hardship near the end of their lives. When the people we have loved reach the boundary of coherence, we can understand the bitterness of Philip Larkin's poem "The Old Fools."

INDEX

A

absolute priority, 89
Achenbaum, Andrew, 209
acute care, 5
adequacy, in social security, 56
age, choices and, 41–42
age group(s)
  defined, 3
  differences between, 210–211
  generations and, 208–212
  generation vs., 3
  justice for, 197–201
  principles of justice for, 17–18
age inequality, 6–9
Alzheimer's disease
  affection and, 178
  autonomy and, 182–185
  critical interests and, 175, 180,
    185–190
  death and, 175–177
  degrees of, 177
  in Dworkin, 173–182
  experience and, 174–175
  goals and, 178–179
  lack of autonomy in, 174–175
  personal identity and, 191–192
  values and, 180–181
  will changes and, 182–183

autonomy
  Alzheimer's disease and, 182–185
  goals and, 178
  lack of, in Alzheimer's, 174–175
  planned death and, 175–176
  precedent, 183
  as value, 173

B

Baby Boomers, 2
Ball, Robert, 12–15
Beauvoir, Simone de, 11
benefit
  egalitarianism and, 57–58
  priority and, 54–55, 91
  simultaneous segments view and, 74
  surplus of, as goal, 120–121
  well-being and, 89
Bengston, Vera, 209
birth cohort, 2
Brock, Dan, 40n2
Broome, John, 94
Bykvist, Krister, 159–161, 165, 167

C

career, priority and, 107
changing places egalitarianism,
    58–59

choices
    age and, 41–42
    contractualism and, 23
    egalitarianism and, 22, 30–31, 76
    goals and, 147–148
    inequality and, 76
    priority and, 103, 121
    prudent insurance ideal and, 39–40
    prudent rationality and, 42–43
comparative value, equality as, 71–72
compensation
    egalitarianism and, 24–25
    equality and, 72, 102–103
    priority and, 101–102, 102–103, 137
    simultaneous segments view and, 73
    time and, 24
complete lives
    egalitarianism, 21–32
    lifespans and, 37
    middle age and, 45
    priority and, 90
    social security and, 202
contractualism, justice and, 22–23
corresponding segments view, 66–67,
    69n16, 71, 99, 127–128
Cowen, Tyler, 41

D

Daniels, Norman, 8, 13–15, 33–38, 40–41,
    43, 43n1, 48–49, 57, 64, 64n12, 79,
    141, 205, 207
death, Alzheimer's disease and, 175–177
decision-making
    age and, 41–42
    contractualism and, 23
    egalitarianism and, 22, 30–31, 76
    goals and, 147–148
    inequality and, 76
    priority and, 103, 121
    prudent insurance ideal and, 39–40
    prudent rationality and, 42–43
dementia, 130–131. *See also* Alzheimer's
    disease
Derthick, Martha, 13n6
distribution
    equality and, 23
    fair, 15

personal identity and, 123, 123n4
    priority and, 100, 111–112
    synchronic, 34, 35
    temporal stages and, 142
    time and, 34
Dresser, Rebecca, 191n8
duration, of inequality, 81–82
Dworkin, Ronald, 24, 38–41, 43, 173–182,
    183–184, 188n6

E

egalitarianism, 16–17
    benefit and, 57–58
    changing places, 58–59
    choices and, 22, 30–31, 76
    compensation and, 24–25
    complete lives, 21–32
    concerns of, 21
    desert and, 198n1
    equality in, 73
    gain and, 120
    history of, 24
    interpersonal judgments and, 25, 138
    intrapersonal choices and, 121
    intrapersonal judgments and, 25, 138
    personal identity and, 82, 115
    priority and, 57–58, 92
    responsibility and, 30–31, 76, 104
    separateness and, 26
    simultaneous segments view and,
        77–78, 83–84, 103
    standard, 25–27
    temporal stages and, 199–200
elderly
    health care consumption by, 5
    priority of, 54
    quality of life of, 6–7
    support for, 1–5
equality
    application of, over time, 60–61
    compensation and, 72, 102–103
    complete lives and, 37
    corresponding segments view and,
        66–67, 69n16, 71, 99, 127–128
    distribution and, 23
    in egalitarianism, 73
    fair distribution and, 15

of opportunity, *vs.* of welfare, 40n2
priority *vs.*, 88, 98, 99, 108
prudential rationality and, 28
as relative value, 71–72
requirement of, 81
simultaneous segments view of, 61,
 62–63, 69–87, 88, 91, 97, 101, 102,
 103, 105, 114, 127–129, 144n9, 215
stages of life and, 53–54
temporal scope of, 21–23
temporal stages and, 61, 99–100
total segments view of, 61, 66–69,
 67n14, 70, 71, 99–100, 128, 129
value of, 98–99
well-being and, 21, 97
equity, in social security, 56
experience, Alzheimer's disease and,
 174–175

F
frame theory of justice, 35, 37, 57, 64, 116
futures, justice and, 14–15

G
generation(s)
 age groups and, 208–212
 age group *vs.*, 3
 as birth cohort, 2
 birth cohort *vs.*, 2
 defined, 2
 differences among, 209–210
 justice between, 6–15
 overview of, 2–3
generational justice, 208–209
goals
 Alzheimer's disease and, 178–179
 autonomy and, 178
 choices and, 147–148
 conflicting, 148–149
 present-aim view and, 155–156
 prudence and, 146–149
 well-being and, 146–147, 166
guild analogy, 8–9

H
health care
 consumption of, by elderly, 5

funding of, 4–5
 practical problems with, 12
 solving problem of, 5
 as transfer of resources from young to
 old, 5
hedonism, well-being and, 168–170
hierarchy, age inequality and, 9
Hurka, Thomas, 107

I
identity
 Alzheimer's disease and, 191–192
 appeal to, 122–134
 dementia and, 130–131
 as different over time, 122
 distribution and, 123, 123n4
 egalitarianism and, 82, 118–121
 identification with other selves and, 130
 in multiple selves analysis, 122
 personal stages and, 118–119
 priority and, 126, 134–136
 problems with appeal to, 125–129,
 130–134
 prudence and, 119, 132
 psychological changes and, 125
 psychological connections and,
 124–125
 revisionist view of, 122, 127
 simultaneous segments view and,
 128–129
 temporal stages and, 118–119, 122
 total segments view and, 128
 weakening of, 118–119
 well-being and, 129
inequality
 age, 6–9
 aging and, 7
 agreement to, by parties, 75
 assessment of, 61
 choices and, 76
 between complete lives, 37
 duration of, 81–82
 guild analogy of, 8–9
 harm in, 72
 leveling down and, 80
 priority and, 100–101
 responsibility and, 76

inequality (*cont.*)
simultaneous, 81
in simultaneous segments view, 71, 79
social security and, 56
temporal stages and, 53–54, 61, 79
time and, 60
wrongfulness of, 72
institutional care, 5
insurance ideal, prudent, 39
interpersonal choices, priority and, 121
interpersonal judgments, 25, 138
interpretational justice, 13
intrapersonal choices, priority and, 121
intrapersonal judgments, 25, 138

J
Jaworska, Agnieszka, 174, 180–181, 187, 188n6
Job (biblical figure), 59, 96–97
judgments
interpersonal, 25, 138
intrapersonal, 25, 138
justice
for age groups, 197–201
contractualism and, 22–23
in Daniels, 13
egalitarianism and, 16–17
frame theory of, 35, 37, 57, 64, 116
futures and, 14–15
generational, 208–209
between generations, 6–15
health care consumption and, 5
interpretational, 13
lifetime perspective on, 11–12
in Nagel, 8–10
principles of, 17–18, 197–198
priority and, 114
simultaneous segments view and, 74
social security and, 4
temporal unit for application of, 9–10
time and, 14–15

K
Kamm, Frances, 112
Kappel, Klemens, 79–81, 111

L
Larkin, Philip, 46–47, 216
Laslett, Peter, 208–209
leveling down, 74, 75, 76, 80, 101, 103, 128,
lifetimes. *See also* temporal stages; time
complete lives and, 37
temporal stages of, comparison of, 52–55
as units, 28–29

M
marriage, 59–60
Mayerfield, Jamie, 135–136
McMahan, Jeff, 124–125, 133, 193–194
middle age, 45
modest objectivism, 148, 150–152, 165–166
momentary suffering, priority and, 101
Moon, Marilyn, 62n10, 66n13
"multiple selves analysis," 122
Murray, Tonya, 209

N
Nagel, Thomas, 9–11, 23, 24, 82–83, 106–107, 137, 151–152, 156, 159, 161, 166
neutrality, temporal, 153–154

O
objectivism, modest, 148, 150–152, 165–166
objectivity, rationality and, 157–158
Old Age (de Beauvoir), 11
"Old Fools, The" (Larkin), 46–47, 216
organ transplant, 112

P
Parfit, Derek, 80, 82, 83, 83n23, 89, 123–124, 133, 152, 154–155, 156, 167
personal identity
Alzheimer's disease and, 191–192
appeal to, 122–134
dementia and, 130–131
as different over time, 122
distribution and, 123, 123n4
egalitarianism and, 82, 118–121
identification with other selves and, 130

in multiple selves analysis, 122
priority and, 126, 134–136
problems with appeal to, 125–129,
    130–134
prudence and, 119, 132
psychological changes and, 125
psychological connections and,
    124–125
revisionist view of, 122, 127
simultaneous segments view and,
    128–129
temporal stages and, 118–119, 122
total segments view and, 128
weakening of, 118–119
well-being and, 129
person stages, 160–161
positive response condition, 149
Posner, Richard, 40, 41, 122
poverty, priority and, 92
precedent autonomy, 183
present, priority and, 112
present-aim theory, 154–155
present-aim view, 154–158, 158–159
principles, of justice, 17–18, 197–198
priority
    absolute, 89
    application of, 90–91
    benefit and, 54–55, 91
    career and, 107
    choices and, 103, 121
    coherence in views of, 94–95
    compensation and, 101–102,
        102–103, 137
    complete lifetimes and, 90
    corresponding segments view and, 99
    distribution and, 100, 111–112
    egalitarianism and, 57–58, 92
    equality vs., 88, 98, 99, 108
    gain and, 108
    inequality and, 100–101
    Job (biblical figure) and, 96–97
    justice and, 114
    momentary suffering and, 101
    personal identity and, 126, 134–136
    poverty and, 92
    present and, 112
    prudence and, 137–145

responsibility and, 104
simplicity of, 110–111
simultaneity and, 101
simultaneous segments view and, 105
social justice and, 115
suffering and, 91–92, 135–136
temporal stages and, 88–89, 96–101, 100
time intervals and, 106
time-neutrality and, 93
time-specific view of, 96–101, 101–110,
    110–117
understanding, 88–96
urgency and, 112
utilitarianism and, 108
utilitarianism vs., 109
value and, 95
well-being and, 54–55, 89–90, 94–95,
    105–106, 135
work and, 107
Proust, Marcel, 1
prudence
    argument for, 47–51
    goals and, 146–149
    modest objectivism and, 150–152
    priority and, 137–145
    social security and, 214–215
    temporal neutrality and, 153–154
    well-being and, 138–139
prudential rationality, 27–28, 34, 42–43
prudential solution, 149–154
prudential thinking, 14
prudent insurance ideal, 39–40

Q
quality of life
    benefit and, 89
    constituents of, 95
    of elderly, 6–7
    equality and, 21, 97
    gain of, 98
    goals and, 146–147
    at particular time, 106
    personal identity and, 129
    positive response condition and, 149
    priority and, 54–55, 89–90, 94–95,
        105–106, 135
    prudence and, 138–139

INDEX

quality of life (*cont.*)
  role of, 162–172
  temporal stages and, 97–98
  value and, 95

R

Rawls, John, 24, 138, 197–198
relations, identity and, 124–125
relative value, equality as, 71–72
responsibility
  egalitarianism and, 30–31, 76, 104
  inequality and, 76
  life stages and, 78–79
  priority and, 104
  simultaneous segments view and, 77
retrospective value enhancement,
    170–171
Ross, W. D., 10n4, 113n9

S

Scanlon, Thomas, 24
Shiffrin, Seana, 174, 179, 192–193
separateness, 26
simplicity, priority and, 110–111
simultaneous inequality, 81
simultaneous segments view, 61, 62–63,
    69–87, 88, 91, 97, 101, 102, 103, 105,
    114, 127–129, 144n9, 215
simultaneous values view, 158–161
slavery, 59
social security
  adequacy of, 56
  complete lives and, 202
  defined, 3
  equity in, 56
  examples of, 3
  fairness and, 212–213
  inequality and, 56
  justice and, 4
  moral complexity of, 206–207
  participation in, 3–4
  "pay as you go" financing for, 3
  practical problems with, 12
  prudence and, 214–215
  Robert Ball on, 12–13
subjectivity, rationality and, 157
synchronic distribution, 34, 35

T

Temkin, Larry, 59, 64, 89
temporal neutrality, 153–154
temporal stages
  comparison of, 52–55
  distribution and, 142
  egalitarianism and, 199–200
  equality and, 61, 99–100
  fairness and, 53–54
  inequality and, 53–54, 61, 79
  personal identity and, 118–119
  priority and, 88–89, 96–101
  well-being and, 97–98
tense, present-aim view and, 158–159
Theory of Justice (Rawls), 24
time
  application of equality over, 60–61
  application of justice and, 9–10
  compensation and, 24
  in Daniels, 33–38
  distribution and, 34
  egalitarianism and, 17
  equality and, 21–23
  inequality and, 60
  justice and, 14–15
  lifetimes as unit of, 28–29
  living in, 1–2
  passage of, 2
  personal identity and, 122
  priority and, 93
  prudential rationality and, 27–28
  -specific view of priority, 96–101,
    101–110, 110–117
total segments view, 61, 66–69, 67n14, 70,
    71, 99–100, 128, 129

U

urgency, priority and, 112
utilitarianism, 46, 108
  gain and, 108–109
  priority and, 108
  priority *vs.*, 109

V

value enhancement, 169–170
values
  Alzheimer's disease and, 180–181

critical interests and, 185–186
present-aim view and, 154–158
simultaneous values view and, 158–161
Velleman, David, 107

W
well-being
  benefit and, 89
  constituents of, 95
  of elderly, 6–7
  equality and, 21, 97
  gain of, 98
  goals and, 146–147, 166

hedonic aspect of, 168–170
objective value determinant of, 164n5
objectivism and, 163
at particular time, 106
personal identity and, 129
positive response condition and, 149
priority and, 54–55, 89–90, 94–95,
  105–106, 135
prudence and, 138–139
role of, 162–172
temporal stages and, 97–98
value and, 95
work, priority and, 107